SHAKESPERE'S HOME

AT

NEW PLACE, STRATFORD-UPON-AVON.

AMS PRESS
NEW YORK

Frontispiece.

"𝔖𝔥𝔞𝔨𝔢𝔰𝔭𝔢𝔯𝔢."

"O on a \ S. a Spear. O. Crest a Falcon, wings display'd,
"A, supporting a Spear in |. O. Granted 20 October, 1596, to
"JOHN SHAKESPERE, of *Stratford-upon-Avon*, in *Com. Warr.*, Gent.,
"per WILL. DETHICK."—(*Index Coll. Arm.*)

SHAKESPERE'S HOME

AT

New Place,

STRATFORD-UPON-AVON.

Being a History of the "Great House" built in the Reign of KING HENRY VII., *by* SIR HUGH CLOPTON, KNIGHT, *and subsequently the property of* WILLIAM SHAKESPERE, GENT., *wherein he lived and died.*

BY

J. C. M. BELLEW.

Imprynted in *London*,
FOR
VIRTUE BROTHERS AND CO.,
1, AMEN CORNER, PATERNOSTER ROW.

MDCCCLXIII.

Library of Congress Cataloging in Publication Data

Bellew, John Chippendall Montesquieu, 1823-1874.
    Shakespere's home at New Place, Stratford-upon-Avon.

    Reprint of the 1863 ed.
    1. Shakespeare, William, 1564-1616--Homes and
haunts--Stratford-upon-Avon. I. Title.
PR2916.B3   1972   822.3'3   76-113553
ISBN 0-404-00736-8

Reprinted from the edition of 1863, London
First AMS edition published in 1972
Manufactured in the United States of America

International Standard Book Number: 0-404-00736-8

AMS PRESS INC.
NEW YORK, N.Y.   10003

TO THE REVEREND

GRANVILLE JOHN GRANVILLE,

B.C.L.,

VICAR OF STRATFORD-UPON-AVON.

---o---

MY DEAR VICAR,

Allow me to Dedicate to you the following Account of NEW PLACE, which would never have been written but for your hofpitality.

To you, and to our friend, Mr. Hunt, I, and a little circle of friends, have, on two occafions, been under great obligations in making pilgrimages to Stratford. If you can fpend half-an-hour pleafantly with me, I hope you will receive my little Book as an affurance of my lively recollection of the happy hours which I have owed to you. That you may, in recruited health, long live to guard that Shrine which is committed to your keeping, and to enjoy the affectionate refpect of your Parifhioners, and troops of Friends, is,

My dear Vicar,

The fincere wifh of

Your much obliged,

J. C. M. BELLEW.

Thames Cottage, Hampton,
New Year's Day, 1863.

PREFACE.

✳✳✳✳✳✳✳✳✳✳✳✳✳✳✳✳✳✳✳✳✳✳✳✳✳✳✳✳✳✳✳✳✳✳✳

ON entering a Continental Cathedral the traveller's attention is arrested by an iron Corona studded with burning tapers. They are the humble offerings of devotees.

The following pages are my humble offering at the shrine of that intellectual edifice, so vast in proportion and so lovely in detail, which our Shakespere erected by his works. Let me stand where the iron Corona does, close to the portal, holding my feet in reverence, and not venturing to tread, with any pretence of critical survey, the long drawn aisles of that stupendous structure which astonishes and delights the master minds of our race.

race. I shall not need to be told that the "farthing-candle ray" is a very appropriate simile to characterise the following pages. It is so. But let me pray that it be not blown out, or snuffed out, with cruel heedlessness (puffed, of course, it is not likely to be), because, though its quantity of illuminating power be but a "little " inch of light," so far as it does extend, I believe it disperses some darkness, and may prove useful in giving other pilgrims to the shrine, a momentary glimpse of dim distances, which may excite curiosity, and the desire to explore their hidden recesses.

In simple language, I believe a great many facts regarding Shakespere remain to be brought to light; and that, while the critic or scholar has little left to say that is fresh or new regarding his works, the antiquary may have a great deal to discover and to say regarding the man.

It

Preface.

It is remarkable what a labour of love has been expended by many eminent men of my own profeſſion upon the works of the Poet. In their wake I have not dared to follow; but I ſhall have done ſome good, I truſt, if I detect a need and point it out, ſo that others, wiſer, and better than I, may provide for its ſatisfaction. The title of my book ſuggeſts a ſubject upon which there reſts the darkneſs of an almoſt profound ignorance. What do we know of the man Shakeſpere in his home—in his domeſtic, ſocial, moral character, in his home aſſociations and his home aſſociates;—nay! what have we *cared* to know of him in them?

Let not the reader be deceived, and tempted into reading my book by ſuppoſing that I pretend to lift the veil, and with my tiny taper to illuminate the darkneſs. I do not. But *I do try to make*

make the darkneſs viſible ; and to the beſt of my opportunities, I have ſtriven to caſt a little light upon ſcattered points, and ſome few facts, which I think have not previouſly been publiſhed.

The ableſt and moſt learned man would ſpeak with modeſty and heſitation regarding any work he might publiſh referring to Shakeſpere. It is with the moſt ſincere diffidence that I venture to let the following pages paſs through the Preſs; but I take courage to do ſo from the belief, that every one who will honour me by reading what I have written, will ſee that I have honeſtly laboured at the facts of my ſubject, and that the opinions I venture to expreſs, are alſo honeſtly put forth.

If I extend this Preface to an inordinate length, it is from my anxiety to have my object underſtood—or, at leaſt, not miſunderſtood.

The

Preface.

The Pedigrees introduced in this work have coſt an infinity of labour, which, the unintereſted or uninitiated, would never ſuppoſe, in glancing over their ſtatiſtical deſcents. It would be unfair to criticiſe them as if they bore the *imprimatur* of a King-at-Arms. Herald's College will only ſmile on them as the productions of a tyro. So they are. But, whatever amount of light they give, the flint and ſteel have been my own.

Ut varias uſus meditando extunderet artes
Paulatim,   *   *   *   *
Et filicis venis abſtruſum excuderet ignem.

I believe I am turning inquiry in a uſeful, and much neglected direction, by preſſing ſuch pedigrees upon the conſideration of thoſe who are curious in Shakeſperian inveſtigations. My reaſons for ſo doing will be found in the body of my work. Whether I have laboured to a purpoſe
and

and done good, or laboured in vain, I leave others to judge.

To the Clopton Pedigree I muſt draw particular attention, and eſpecially to that branch of it referring to the Combes family. In the Appendix (Article, " Combes ") the reader will learn the difficulties and perplexities encountered: and will, I am certain, give me credit for a painſtaking purſuit of my object, and hold me pardonable if I ſhould be found hereafter to have made any miſtakes. In the Appendix, likewiſe, will be found many curious facts reflecting upon the perſons to whom reference is made, which I conſidered could not be legitimately introduced into the body of my work. The ſingular diſcovery made, with regard to the man Bott (Appendix A, p. 341), will explain how it came to paſs that New Place was originally ſold.

"*Qui ſ'excuſe, ſ'accuſe !*" If ſo, my
excuſes

excufes muft amount to felf-accufation; but of one thing I do not accufe myfelf, and that is, of thankleffnefs to the various friends who have given me their help. To Mr. T. Duffus Hardy, Deputy Keeper of Public Records; Mr. Burtt, and Mr. Cole of the Record Office; to Mr. Planché and his *confrères* at Herald's College; to the Vicar of Stratford, his Curates, and William Butcher, the Parifh Clerk; to Mr. Clarence Hopper, in making a variety of refearches for me; to Mr. Hunt, Town Clerk of Stratford, in patiently enduring my endlefs letters and inquiries;—to thefe gentlemen, and to a number of others, whofe kindnefs has had my private thanks, (becaufe they object to being mentioned here,) I am greatly and fincerely indebted. Let me offer my thanks likewife to another perfon. To John Middleton, Attendant in the Reading-Room of the Britifh Mufeum,

not

not only of late, but for years, I have been indebted for conftant attention. I thank him moft heartily; and think I do myfelf honour when I go a ftep out of my way to mark the obligations, which thofe who frequent the Britifh Mufeum, the Record Office, the Will Office, and all other fuch public inftitutions, owe to the courtefy always extended to readers and fearchers, not only by the fuperior officers of thofe places, but alfo by their humbler affiftants.

I fhall be pleafed, if, on clofing my book, any of my readers feel a frefhened intereft in the *Man*—William Shakefpere; and above all, I fhall be beft fatisfied if they are led to think with me, that this Prince of Poets was a worthier and better man than we vulgarly account him; that Shakefpere's Home is a fubject deferving our ftudy and refpect; and that he was no hypocritical mouther of fine fenti-
ments

ments, inditing with his pen the nobleſt and loftieſt teaching, and belying it in the conduct of his life.

I conceive that no one can teach effectively, that which he has not himſelf felt earneſtly; nor until good can be put for evil, and evil for good, can I bring myſelf to think that the pureſt intellectual refreſhment of a race thirſting after knowledge, pours from a polluted ſource. I picture Shakeſpere to myſelf as an embodiment of the manly, honeſt, and lofty virtues, which his Muſe delights to crown with honour; and half my reverence for him would be gone if I did not feel morally convinced that the greateſt of all human teachers, was not only a Great Man, but alſo a Good Man!

⁎ As Shakeſpere's name has been ſpelt by ſo many different people in ſo many different ways, I may remark that the orthography I have adopted is that of the Grant of Arms in Herald's College, 1596; believing, as I do, that the ſpelling in that document was dictated by Shakeſpere to Dethick.

CORRIGENDA.

———o———

Page 205.—" no one could," read " no one would."

Page 205.—" Gilrow," read " Gildon."

Page 218.—" thofe years enjoying," read " thofe years *as* enjoying."

Page 230.—" Revels," read " Revel."

NEW PLACE,

Stratford-upon-Avon.

✱✱✱✱✱✱✱✱✱✱✱✱✱✱✱✱✱✱✱✱✱✱✱✱✱✱✱✱✱✱✱✱

"ON the north side of this Chapell
"was a Fair House, built of brick
"and timber, by the said Hugh, wherein
"he lived in his later dayes and dyed.
"On the south side of which Chapell
"stands the Grammar School." These
words, quoted from Dugdale's "War-
"wickshire," and referring to Sir Hugh
Clopton, Knt., were, until the other day,
the chief record possessed by Englishmen
of

of the houfe in which William Shakefpere alfo "lived in his later days, and "died." At length the ftones prate of his whereabout, and it feems defirable to lay their information before the public.

Every one, even remotely interefted in the fubject, is aware, that a fhort time back, the land on which Shakefpere's houfe was known to have ftood (ufually denominated "Shakefpere's Garden," and, as fuch, pointed out to perfons vifiting Stratford-upon-Avon,) was for fale. It is equally well known that an appeal was made to the public by Mr. Halliwell [*vide The Times*, October 15, 1861], and that the plot of land in queftion, was refcued from the grafp of private fpeculators, or fhowmen, to be vefted in the charge of truftees, and by them to be preferved for ever—fet apart, and, in effect, confecrated to the memory of the man who lived there, happily accordant with

with the prayer expreſſed in Garrick's words:—

> "*And may no sacrilegious hand*
> *Near Avon's banks be found,*
> *To dare to parcel out the land,*
> *And limit Shakespere's hallowed ground.*
> *For ages free, still be it unconfined,*
> *As broad and general as thy boundless mind.*"

As ſoon as the ſympathy of the public for the object in queſtion was exhibited, the ambition of its promoters expanded as the ſubſcriptions increaſed; and nothing leſs than the full and entire recovery of the eſtate once poſſeſſed by Shakeſpere at New Place, would ſatisfy theſe ardent and enthuſiaſtic individuals.

Goldſmith complained (to Dodſley after dinner) that his was an "unpoetic "age." There are many chatterers of the preſent day who repeat the complaint, which ſeems to have become ſtereotyped for all time. It was a fooliſh thought

thought to say "an unpoetic age," for every age must seem to the men of the day matter of fact and unpoetic. To-day always appears prosaic; yesterday and to-morrow—subjects of retrospection and anticipation, not objects in possession—are the fit themes for poetry. Goldsmith's age, however prosaic it may have seemed, gave *him* good proof of its poetic appreciation; and so our age (iron age though it may be) gives equally good proof of its admiration for the real poet and for genuine poetry, wherever it finds the one, or reads the other.

If the true poet lives in the hearts and memories of his countrymen, how much more the Prince of all the Bards?

There are those who will boldly assert that Shakespere's works do not attract, and that people generally, care little or nothing about Shakespere himself. It is not to the purpose in this place to enter
into

into any discussion upon such topics. It might, however, be argued that the students of his works have found themselves compelled (unless contented with being guilty of ignorance) to make the Poet's plays the companions of the closet; and that from the student's closet the most valuable interpretations of his text have issued of late years. Such an argument would infer that the marvellous creations of the Poet's mind command peculiar respect at the present time; and it may be unhesitatingly asserted, that abundant evidence is forthcoming to prove that this is a fact. There has not been an era in English literature more fruitful in labours of critical comment upon the text of Shakespere, and more inquiring into every sort of evidence likely to throw light upon his life and history. It might also be argued, that the people of England are

just

just as proud of, and juft as interefted in, the fame of their countryman—are juft as anxious to preferve with facred care every relique and memento of the brighteft genius the world has ever produced, as any of their forefathers have been. Circumftances, perhaps, would warrant the affertion that the prefent generation exhibits more intereft in him, and more reverence for everything connected with him, than any other fince his death. The fentiment of George II., that Shakefpere's plays are bombaft, no longer commands courtly acquiefcence; and the Carlton Houfe fafhion of depreciating his works (particularly by thofe who had never ftudied them) is a fafhion that has had its day. Doubtlefs, the confervative feeling of this period with reference to the Poet's birthplace, his laft refidence, and the few reliques connected with him that furvive, has been operated upon by
that

that revival of taſte for architecture, and that reverence for mediæval art, which does honour to the reign of Victoria, and will hereafter ſignaliſe it. The hiſtorian will tell how, from the ſixteenth to the nineteenth century, the eccleſiaſtical architecture of England univerſally, and the domeſtic generally, became baſer and ſtill more baſe; until, towards the cloſe of the Georgian era, it reached a depth of degradation (land-marked by the introduction of Roman Cement and Cockney Villas) than which nothing could be more infamous. The ſame hiſtorian will tell of the great work that Pugin did, of the conſequent refuſcitation of taſte, and of love for architectural beauty becoming a neceſſary part of polite education. He will tell how (as the legitimate accompaniments of ſuch regenerated refinement) the Engliſh people awoke to the conviction that the fabrics of their churches

had

had been at the mercy of Goths and Vandals, and that the moſt intereſting hiſtorical remains of domeſtic architecture had been ſhameleſsly deſtroyed or barbarouſly mutilated. Then came the Reſtoration: a reſtoration in its particular province more beneficial and remedial than ſome chronological events deſignated by that phraſe have proved.

To the therapeutic ſpirit, ſo happily prevalent in England at the preſent period regarding mediæval art, may fairly be attributed ſome meaſure of the intereſt, and a great amount of the funds, which have been ſubſcribed to reſtore the birthplace of Shakeſpere, in Henley Street, at Stratford; and alſo to ſave his laſt place of reſidence from being utiliſed for "build-"ing lots," or vulgariſed by any ſpeculative Barnum.

For ſome months the ſubject has dropped out of public notice. The terrific calamity

calamity at Hartley Colliery, and the incumbent subscriptions of all generous and charitable people, for the widows and orphans of the deceased; the heavy visitation upon the Queen and country, followed by the Memorial Fund; and last of all, the increasing want of our long-suffering and brave fellow-countrymen in Lancashire, calling for the admiration and sympathetic contributions of those who can aid them in their dire necessity, have, for a period, checked any appeals to public sympathy, except those of an urgent character.

In the face of such griefs and such wants, it was impossible for the Shakespere Fund subscription list to keep its place before the public. It has, probably for this reason, been temporarily withdrawn. If so, the act has been judicious. While the subject is in abeyance, it may be well to consider what has been done
with

with the money subscribed, because a judicious expenditure already made, would be the best basis of appeal to the public for further moneys to meet future outlays.

It is familiar to every one, that Shakespere's residence at Stratford was called "New Place." There are popular errors in existence, both about the place, and the name of the place. It may be acceptable to the reader if a few facts are thrown together to tell its history, which will be no information to those who have been interested in New Place, but may be instructive to many not "read up" in the subject.

New Place came from, and returned to, the family of Clopton. The Cloptons possessed it long prior to Shakespere's time, and repossessed it by intermarriage (subsequent to Shakespere's time) with a daughter of Sir Edward Walker.

Dugdale (as quoted) states that the house

OCKWELLS, BERKSHIRE.

house was built by Sir Hugh Clopton, of brick and timber. Sir Hugh lived in the reign of Henry VII. The general appearance of the building can be easily imagined, though *there is no drawing of it in existence.*

The plate on the opposite page gives a representation of a house built about the same time that Sir Hugh Clopton erected " New Place." It presents to us the front elevation of " Ockwells," in the parish of Bray, Berkshire, at present possessed by Mr. Grenfell, of Taplow. This house is stated to have been built during the reign of Richard III., and is one of the very few specimens of *domestic architecture* now remaining of that date. The Great Hall, until lately, was adorned by a beautiful stained-glass window, emblazoned with the armorial bearings of Henry VII., and the Duke of Somerset; but, in a spirit akin to Vandalism, this most interesting remnant

nant of antique heraldry has been removed from its proper place, and fixed up in Mr. Grenfell's new houfe, on Taplow Hill. It will not furprife the public, knowing this fact, to learn that Ockwells is turned into an ordinary farm-houfe; that its architectural intereft and artiftic beauty, as well as antiquity, are apparently unappreciated; and that its noble hall, with open-worked Gothic roof and oak wainfcoting, is made a ploughboy's lumber-room, filled with agricultural implements, ploughs, fpades, facks, barrows, and rakes.* The accompanying drawing of Ockwells has been given in order to prefent a faithful reprefentation of a "great houfe, built of wood and timber," of the time of Henry VII. It is only to be

---

* An unfatisfactory hiftory of the houfe, accompanied with two admirable drawings of the window referred to, will be found in Lyfon's "Magna Britannica," Berkfhire, Bray, parifh of.

be regarded as a fpecimen of a period, from which Sir Hugh Clopton's houfe would no doubt differ greatly in detail, but with which it would agree in character and effect.

The lovers of "illuftrated works" have been indulged with a plate reprefenting Shakefpere's houfe at New Place; but a drawing of a caftle in the air would have been equally authoritative and correct. This is one error concerning New Place that needs to be exploded. No authentic reprefentation of it exifts. When Dugdale ufes the words "brick "and timber," and tells us that the houfe was built in the reign of Henry VII., any one who has vifited Coventry, Chefter, Shrewfbury, or the "Mint" at Briftol, will be able, in his mind's eye, to picture the general appearance of Shakefpere's houfe, with its multiplied gables, its overhanging eaves, its barge-boards, enriched

with

with the Tudor flower-ornament (as at the Coventry Almſhouſe), its projecting windows, its ſtrong framework of croſs-beamed, black, old Engliſh oak forming the ribs or ſkeleton of the houſe, the intervening ſquares built in with brick (probably plaſtered over and whitewaſhed), its wooden porchway, open-arcaded, with a room above, whoſe oriel windows diſplayed the falcon and tilting ſpear.

Of that houſe, which Sir Hugh Clopton built, and in which Shakeſpere ſubſequently lived and died, not a veſtige remained but yeſterday. Like the inſubſtantial pageant (of the Poet's play), not a rack was left behind, as far as any living man could tell.

Shakeſpere's Barn may, in a certain ſenſe, be ſaid to have exiſted up to 1861. In that year a couple of cottages occupying that portion of New Place garden which adjoins the theatre on the weſt,
were

were taken down, having, in the first instance, been photographed, and then stripped to the framework of which they were constructed. These cottages had been contrived by subdividing the ancient barn belonging to Shakespere. On removing the thatch, the lath and plaster work from between the beams, and reducing the building to its skeleton structure, it was found that, in the lapse of two centuries and a half, all the timbers of the barn had, from time to time, been replaced, with the exception of some three or four small beams. These were the sole remains of the Poet's Barn.

The recent purchase of New Place led to a series of excavations, and the discoveries which have resulted, (though not very extensive,) are extremely interesting, and definitely settle several points which, heretofore, have been subjects of surmise and speculation.

The

The leading facts regarding New Place are these:

1st. New Place was built by Sir Hugh Clopton, *temp.* Henry VII., *circ.* 1490. He died in London, 1496, and being a bachelor, devised it to his great-nephew, William Clopton, who died in 1521.

2nd. From the Clopton family it passed by purchase to the family of Bott, in the reign of Queen Elizabeth, 1563.*

3rd. By Willian Bott it was resold to Wm. Underhill, within a short space of time, between 1563 and 1570.†

4th. William Shakespere purchased from the Underhill family, for £60, New Place, consisting of " one messuage, " two barns, and two gardens, with " their appurtenances," during the Easter Term of 1597, in the 39th year of the reign of Queen Elizabeth,

---

* Appendix A. † Appendix B.

beth, and the year after his only fon, Hamnet, had died. By him it was repaired, renovated, and fitted up for his permanent refidence.

5th. March, 1616. Shakefpere made his will, leaving it to his daughter, Mrs. Hall, for life; after her, to her daughter. The month following, April 23, 1616, his reputed birthday, he died in this houfe, and was buried two days later, on the 25th, in the 53rd year of his age.

It was a happy accident that the reign of Queen Elizabeth had begun before the birth of the Poet, otherwife this country would have loft the moft valuable records regarding him. As foon as the Queen afcended the throne, the regiftries of the parifh churches were carefully kept. The Regifter-book of Stratford Church contains entries both of the baptifm and the funeral of Shakefpere.

" 1564,

"1564, April 26. Gulielmus, Filius "Johannes Shakſpere." But this merely records his baptiſm, and not the date of birth, which baptiſmal regiſters have never done, and even now do not, although the value of ſuch entries is apparent.

The entry of the funeral runs thus :— 1616, "April 25, Will. Shakſpeare, Gent."

6th. Mrs. Hall ſucceeded to the property, and from her it paſſed to her daughter Elizabeth, Lady Barnard.

7th. Lady Barnard (Shakeſpere's granddaughter) according to an indenture dated 20th October, 1652, covenanted that New Place ſhould be had to the uſe of herſelf and her huſband, John Barnard, during their natural lives, and in default of iſſue, ſhould be left to the uſe of ſuch perſon or perſons as ſhe ſhould limit or appoint. Lady Barnard executed a will, 29th January, 1669, whereby New

Stratford-upon-Avon.

New Place was left to Sir John Barnard for his life, and to the ufe of his executors for fix months after his death. Lady Barnard died a few days afterwards, and was buried at Abington, February 17th, 1669. Her will was proved 4th March, 1669. The property continued in the poffeffion of Sir John until his death in 1673; fubfequent to which, according to the provifions of the aforefaid will, New Place was fold. An indenture, dated 18th May, 1675, conveyed it "to bee and "enure to the only ufe and behoofe "of Sir Edward Walker, Knt., "Garter Principall King at Armes," who completed the purchafe for the fum of £1,060.* He died, as the monument in Stratford Church ftates, the following year—February, 1676. 8th.

---

* Appendix C.

20 *New Place,*

8th. The only child of Sir Edward Walker, Barbara,* married Sir John Clopton,

---

* A native poet of Stratford, by name John Jordan, and by trade a wheelwright, publiſhed in 1777 a poem entitled " Welcombe Hills " (which are in the neighbourhood of Stratford). In alluſion to one of the Clopton marriages—that of Edward (the iſſue of the above Sir John and Barbara his wife) with Martha Combe, the laſt perſon of note of the family of John a Combe (Shakeſpere's friend)—the poet exclaims:—

" *Till a late failure in the iſſue male,*
Turn'd, though unprejudiced, the lineal ſcale,
An heireſs Combe, right well to be ally'd,
Became the heir of neighb'ring Clopton's bride."

As Mrs. Partheriche, the deſcendant of this alliance, will be alluded to, the marriages are here ſubjoined, though the Pedigree of Clopton, *in extenſo,* will be found elſewhere.

Sir Edward Walker.
|
Barbara Walker = Sir John Clopton.
|
Edward Clopton = Martha Combe, last of the line of John a Combe.
|
Edward Clopton = Martha, *d.* of Thomas Middleton, Esq., of Mundham, Surrey.

1 2 3 4 5 6   7
| | | | | | |
Children deceased while young.   Frances Clopton, = John Partheriche, Esq. the last of her family. She survived her husband. *D.* 1793.

Clopton, of Clopton, in the parifh of Stratford, and thus New Place returned again into the Clopton family. Sir John deceafed, April 18, 1719. By him New Place was bequeathed

9th. To his younger fon, Sir Hugh Clopton, of the Middle Temple, one of the Heralds of the College of Arms, and Recorder of Stratford.

10th. Sir Hugh Clopton *pulled down* New Place, *entirely rebuilt* it, and died in the *new New Place*, 1751, aged 80.—*Temp*. George II.

11th. Sir Hugh's fon-in-law and executor Henry Talbot (brother of the Chancellor Talbot), fold it to the Rev. Francis Gaftrell, 1753.

12th. Gaftrell deftroyed the modern houfe, and razed it to the ground, in 1759.

13th.

13th. The subsequent history of New Place—1775 to 1862—may be told in a few words. Mrs. Gastrell sold the property to W. Hunt,* Esq., of Stratford, in 1775.

14th. The trustees under the will of W. Hunt, on the 29th Sept., 1790, sold to Charles Henry Hunt,† Esq., who subsequently purchased of Fanny Mortiboys, spinster, the adjoining house, now known as " Nashe's " House." ‡

15th. The assignees of C. H. Hunt, on the 15th May, 1807, conveyed the whole of the property described upon

---

* Grandfather of W. O. Hunt, Esq., the present Town-clerk of Stratford. He was a promoter of the Jubilee of 1769. Garrick corresponded with him.

† The second son of the aforesaid W. Hunt.

‡ It is only during the present year that it has been ascertained that this house belonged to Thomas Nashe, who married Shakespere's grand-daughter, Elizabeth Hall.

GROUND PLAN of NEW PLACE and the GREAT GARDEN.

upon the Ground Plan as "New "Place," including that now occupied by the "Theatre," to Edmund Batterſbee and William George Morris, Eſqs., Bankers.

16th. In January, 1829, the heir-at-law of E. Batterſbee, and the aſſignees of W. G. Morris, *ſold off the property in lots.*

A—including Naſhe's houſe, was purchaſed by Miſs Lucy Smith.

B—the Cottages formed out of Shakeſpere's Barn, were purchaſed, the one by Michael Prentice, the other by Thomas Webb.

C—the Great Garden (now a Bowling Green), including the ground now occupied by the Theatre, was purchaſed by Edward Leyton.

D—is a ſtrip of land which formerly belonged to the Clifford Charity, and was

was acquired by an exchange effected by Mr. Gaftrell. It never belonged to the Great Garden in Shakefpere's time, though it has continued a part of it fince Mr. Gaftrell acquired it.

E—is a ftrip of Garden at the back of Nafhe's houfe, which always belonged to Nafhe's houfe until 1790, when it was purchafed by C. H. Hunt, and became an integral part of lot A, of which it has ever fince continued a part.

F—is the ruins of foundations lately uncovered, in which is identified a fmall portion of Sir Hugh Clopton's "Great Houfe" of New Place, and a much larger portion of the fecond houfe, built about 1720 (paragraph 10).

17th. In 1834, the faid Edward Leyton purchafed Webb's cottage, and in 1838 he alfo purchafed Prentice's;
fo

so that he became poſſeſſor of the whole of the two lots B and C.

18th. On the 23rd of January, 1836, the truſtees of the above-mentioned Lucy Smith, under her will, ſold the lot A to Mr. David Rice, Surgeon. Some time about this period, between 1836 and 1844, Edward Leyton ſold that portion of the Great Garden whereon the Theatre now ſtands, for the erection of that moſt hideous ſtructure. By the knowledge of this fact, the reader will ſee what amount of " vene- " ration " a ſtaring brick building, raiſed leſs than thirty years ago, can claim from the public.

19th. In July, 1844, the only daughter and child of Edward Leyton, contracted marriage with Chas. Frederic Loggin. Mr. Leyton then ſettled the whole of the remainder of lots B and C

B and C to himself for life, to his wife after him for her life, and after her, to his daughter, under trustees, for her life, *giving them power to sell.*

20th. We are thus brought down to the present period, and to the last sales that will ever occur upon the New Place estate.

A was purchased by Mr. Halliwell, by private contract, of the trustees under the will of the above-named surgeon, Mr. Rice, for the sum of £1,200. It was conveyed 21st March, 1862.

B and C were purchased by Mr. Halliwell, by private contract, of the trustees under the settlement of Mr. Loggin, for £2,000. They were conveyed February 8, 1862.

Accordingly, there still remains to be purchased that piece of ground whereon the theatre stands, sold off from the
Great

Great Garden a few years ago. This "theatre" (fo called) belongs, at the prefent moment, to a body of fhareholders, who are prepared to fell their rights—the ground, buildings, &c.—for £1,100. No doubt this purchafe will, at no diftant period, be made; and then the whole New Place property will belong to the public, vefted in the corporation of Stratford, to be preferved by them for ever, for the contemplation and enjoyment of the Englifh people.

The above detailed facts have been arranged in paragraphs, fo that the reader may, with greater eafe, carry in memory the changes and chances to which New Place has been fubjected.

The familiar entries in the church books of Stratford regarding Shakefpere's baptifm and burial having been given, it will render the fubject more complete if the

the principal facts regarding his marriage, and the issue of that marriage, are added in this place; for it can scarcely be doubted that Shakespere purchased New Place in order to provide a home for his wife and children during his long absences in London—a home which he laboured hard to sustain—a home to which he always retired when the seasons of temporary repose arrived; when, being set free from the mental and physical exertions necessary to carry on the business of Blackfriars and the Globe Theatre, he could enjoy (as he ever loved to do) the sweet associations of that home, and the delights of the Garden of England—the luxuriant valley of the Avon.

Numberless efforts have been made to discover the registry of Shakespere's wedding. Up to the present time, all such efforts have proved vain. The probability—almost the certainty—is, that it has

has long since perished. His marriage bond and licence (bearing date 1582) are preserved at Worcester among the archives of the diocese. They run thus:—

"Noverint universi per presentes nos
"ffulconem Sandells de Stratford in comi-
"tatu Warwici agricolam, et Johannem
"Rychardson ibidem agricolam, teneri
"et firmiter obligari Ricardo Cosin gene-
"roso et Roberto Warmstry notario pub-
"lico in quadraginta libris bonæ et
"legalis monetæ Angliæ solvend, eisdem
"Ricardo et Roberto hæred. execut. vel.
"assignat suis, ad quam quidem solu-
"cionem bene et fideliter faciend, obli-
"gamus nos, et utrumque nostrum per
"se pro toto et in solice hæred, executor
"et administrator, nostros firmiter, per
"præsentes sigillis nostris sigillit. Dat.
"28 die Novem. anno regni Dominæ
"nostræ, Eliz. Dei gratia Angliæ, Ffrancæ,
"et

"et Hiberniæ Reginæ, Fidei Defensor,
"&c., 25°."

"The condicion of this obligacion ys
"suche, that if hereafter there shall not
"appere any lawfull lett or impediment
"by reason of any precontract, consan-
"guitie, affinitie, or by any other lawfull
"meanes whatsoever, but that William
"Shagspere one thone partie, and Ann
"Hathwey, of Stratford, in the dioces of
"Worcester, maiden, may lawfully solem-
"nize matrimony together, and in the
"same afterwardes remaine and continew
"like man and wiffe, according unto the
"lawes in that behalf provided; and,
"moreover, if there be not at this
"present time any action, sute, quarrell,
"or demaund, moved or depending before
"any judge, ecclesiasticall or temporall,
"for and concerning any suche lawfull
"lett or impediment; and, moreover, if
"the

Stratford-upon-Avon. 31

"the faid William Shagfpere do not pro-
"ceed to folemnizacion of mariadg with
"the faid Ann Hathwey without the
"confent of his frindes; and alfo if the
"faid William do, upon his own proper
"coftes and expenfes, defend and fave
"harmles, the Right Reverend Father in
"God, Lord John, Bufhop of Worcefter,
"and his offycers, for licencing them the
"faid William and Ann to be maried
"together with once afking of the bannes
"of matrimony betwene them, and for
"all other caufes which may enfue by
"reafon or occafion thereof, that then
"the faid obligacion to be voyd and of
"none effect, or els to ftand and abide in
"full force and vertue."

Here follow the fignatures, or *marks*, of the witneffes; the firft refembling the attempt that an aged perfon would make to draw a triangle; the fecond being a clumfy letter C. Two feals are added:
the

the one is defaced, the other bears the impression "R. H." Who was "R. H.?" Could this be the seal of the bride's father, Richard Hathaway? and instead of the licence being procured in secresy, as Mr. Collier has suggested, may it not have been granted with the full knowledge and consent of Richard Hathaway? Even supposing that there might be truth in the view which De Quincey and Mr. Collier have taken of this marriage—that it was accomplished hurriedly and secretly—such an argument would strengthen the supposition that "R. H." was the bride's father, and that he had accompanied Shakespere to Worcester, in order to see that the licence was duly secured. Such a supposition would be most natural if there was any ground for scandal, which many persons have shown a singular fancy for insinuating. The "mature young "woman, five years past her maturity,"

being

Stratford-upon-Avon.

being "led aftray by the boy with two "and a half years to run of his minority," is objectionable to De Quincey's contemplation. Perhaps the idea is more abfurd than objectionable.

The evidence of "legal documents"—"a ftory fo fignificant and fo eloquent to "the intelligent,"—certainly fhows that Shakefpere procured his licenfe, 28th November, 1582, and that his firft child, Sufannah, was baptifed the following 26th May, 1583. But what then? Did the mature young woman lead the boy aftray; and did the indignant R. H., on difcovering the truth, infift upon an immediate marriage, to hide his child's difgrace?

This would be one way of explaining the procuring of the licenfe; and there might then be great fignificance in the feal of "R. H." appended to the bond!

It has been conclufively fhown, from the

the very regifters of Stratford, that marriages, with the fame "fignificance of "dates" between the church ceremony and the baptifm of the eldeft child, were cuftomary at Stratford.

It has alfo been fhown, that they were cuftomary in England, and on the continent; and before any fcandal was hinted at, as to the purity of the "mature young "woman," it would have been well for the marriage cuftoms of the age, and of people in Shakefpere's rank of life, to have been carefully ftudied. Even in this nineteenth century, there are ruftic parts of northern England, in which the fnort of the iron-horfe has never been heard, where fuch primitive cuftoms ftill furvive, and contracts of marriage are made precifely as they were in Shakefpere's day.

In fuch bucolic, or, as they might be called, "uncivilifed" parts, marriage
is

is "honourable among all men," and as duly celebrated as the contract is made.

> "*Is it a custom?*
> *Ay, marry, is 't.*"

It is difficult to understand how a youth of Shakespere's age, and of his disposition, could be suspected of secretly and suddenly binding, "in the prayers of holy "church," a connection that he had formed shamefully. Reverence for the memory of so great a moralist, and so warm a champion of female purity and innocence, should prompt every examiner of his life and acts, to compare those acts with the habits and customs of the days in which he lived. Knowing what were the marriage customs common among the folk with whom the poet was early associated, and seeing that his marriage was in accordance with their habits, it is most natural, and certainly most charitable,

able, to suppose that friends like John Shakespere and Richard Hathaway should be well pleased for their families to be connected in marriage. That Ann Hathaway was older than William Shakespere might be her misfortune, but was not her fault. The "mature young "woman" could not help herself; and possibly she may have been kept under her father's roof, denied to the swains of Shottery, waiting until such time as young William Shakespere could, with any propriety, marry. At length the heads of houses agreed that they might be contracted; there was a pleasant trip to Worcester for the licence; "R. H." went to see that everything was done duly and in order; William and Ann were married,—and, it is to be hoped, "they lived "happily ever after."

We are indebted to the antiquarian, Sir Robert Philipps, for discovering the bond

Stratford-upon-Avon.

bond and licenſe in 1836, in the Confiſtorial Court of Worceſter. In the original it is full of legal abbreviations, as given in Mr. Knight's Biography. For the ſake of ſimplicity, the full text, as rendered by Mr. Halliwell, has been adopted above.

The probability is, that the ceremony of marriage was performed in the Chapel of Luddington, a hamlet of the pariſh of Stratford, at a ſhort diſtance from Shottery, the reſidence of Ann Hathaway, and a place with which the Hathaways were connected. The Marquis of Hertford, to whom Luddington belonged, informed Malone that he remembered there were tenants of the name of Hathaway on the eſtate. One, John Hathaway, farmed part of the eſtate as late as 1775. It is alſo worthy of note that the curate of Luddington was the Rev. Thomas Hunt, who was ſchoolmaſter of Stratford

Stratford School when Shakespere would almost certainly be a pupil there.* If the master and pupil were good friends, the fact might be a strong inducement to Shakespere to be married at Mr. Hunt's church. Licenses granted for the parish of Stratford, would, of course, be available for all churches and chapels within the parish, at which marriages were allowed. Luddington Chapel was taken down many years ago, and its registers have either been destroyed or lost.

The annexed Pedigree will give all necessary particulars regarding Shakespere's family, his marriage, and his issue. Writers upon this subject have commonly stated the marriages and descents in the ordinary letterpress of their works, which, in such matters, is confusing.

---

* Masters of the School:—1570, Walter Roche; 1572 to 1577, Thomas Hunt (buried at Stratford, April 12, 1612); 1580, Thomas Jenkins.

fusing. Where a Pedigree is set out, the eye instructs the memory much more easily and directly, and for this reason the present method has been adopted.

Allusion has been made to a popular error regarding Shakespere's residence. Paragraph 10 (p. 21) states that the house in which he lived was pulled down at the commencement of the last century. Any representation of that house, to be authentic, must therefore bear date previous to 1719. No such plate or picture exists, and there is no evidence of any such having existed. In order to satisfy public curiosity, two were invented; the one published by Malone, the other by Samuel Ireland, father of the notorious forger of Vortigern and other Shakesperian MSS. Malone's picture was a draft upon imagination, drawn by John Jordan, of Stratford, to whom reference has been made. Jordan was perfectly prepared,

prepared, for a confideration, to invent or compofe, or make himfelf generally ufeful. In firft publifhing Jordan's reprefentation of New Place, Malone accompanied the drawing with this title, giving it a place in his book, but preferving a complete filence himfelf as to the value or authenticity of the drawing:—

"New Place, from a drawing in the "margin of an ancient furvey, made by "order of Sir George Carew, (afterwards "Baron Carew of Clopton, and Earl of "Totnefs,) and found at Clopton, near "Stratford-upon-Avon, in 1786."

Jordan fubfequently confeffed that he had invented the porch of the houfe; and Malone himfelf approved of his adding Shakefpere's arms, becaufe "*they were* "*very likely to have been there;*" fuggefting, at the fame time, "neat wooden "pales, which might be placed with pro- "priety before the houfe." Ireland, in his

Stratford-upon-Avon. 41

his work upon the Avon, produced an engraving of the houfe, which he boldly afferted was authentic, and taken from a drawing in the poffeffion of Mrs. Partheriche, of Clopton Houfe, the laft of the Clopton family, *which drawing, however, had unfortunately been deftroyed!* His words are as follows :—

"I have taken the liberty of giving a
"view of the houfe as it ftood at the
"time he refided there, which he did
"from the period of his quitting London
"till his death. The view is copied
"from an old drawing of one Robert
"Trefwells, made in 1599, by order of
"Sir George Carew, afterwards Baron
"Carew of Clopton, and Earl of Totnefs.
"It was found in Clopton Houfe in
"1786, and was in the poffeffion of the
"late Mrs. Patriche, who was the laft of
"the antient family of the Clopton's.
"The drawing, I am informed, is fince
"loft

"loft or deftroyed." Whether deftroyed before Ireland made his copy, he omits to mention; but it is of no particular confequence, as the impudent attempt at impofition betrays itfelf.

In the ftatements fet forth by Malone and by Ireland, it is impoffible to overlook thefe facts: they both affert that the drawing was found in the year 1786, and they both ufe the identical words, "made by order of Sir George Carew, "afterwards Baron Carew of Clopton, "and Earl of Totnefs."

Three improvements of the ftory are introduced by Ireland, who favours us with the extra information that the drawing was made by one Robert Trefwells; that it was made in 1599, and that it was in the poffeffion of Mrs. Partheriche, the laft of the Cloptons. Defpite thefe additional baits to beguile the public, and give the ftory an increafed air of truth, it is impoffible

Stratford-upon-Avon. 43

poffible to avoid the impreffion that Ireland was pirating Jordan's invention; and that while he was pointing a moral for future writers, he was adorning a tale at the moment to anfwer his own purpofes.

On comparing the drawings given by Malone and by Ireland, it is palpable that the one is a very slightly altered copy of the other, or that they are both copies of fome third drawing. If a third—poffibly genuine—drawing had exifted, fuch as Malone afferted, and Ireland reafferted, did exift, executed at the inftance of Baron Carew, it is evident that fuch drawing would not have exhibited a porch of Wren's era (*temp.* Charles II.) ftuck in front of a drawing made in 1599 (*temp.* Elizabeth). But we have Jordan's confeffion that "he added the "porch." A genuine drawing, therefore, in the poffeffion of Mrs. Partheriche, would have been minus the porch which
Jordan

Jordan added, and minus the arms upon that porch, which Malone approved, becaufe "they were very likely to have been "there." What fhall be thought, then, of Ireland's picture, which prefents to us the confeffed impofition practifed by Jordan, and improved upon by Malone?

There can be very little doubt that Ireland took Malone's drawing, added barge-boards to it, and reproduced it as copied from an original at Clopton Houfe.

Two queftions of intereft ftill remain to be afked. Did any fuch drawing ever exift on the margin of a furvey? If fuch did not exift, how came it that Malone lent himfelf to the impudent invention of Jordan, and publifhed it as genuine, knowing that in fome refpects Jordan had "improved" it?

It is hard to believe that any fuch drawing exifted—certainly not as defcribed by Malone, on the authority of Jordan—

becaufe

becaufe a furvey of his property, made by Lord Carew in 1599, would not be a furvey of other people's eftates. Lord Carew was contemporary with Shakefpere, and might have known that New Place belonged to him two years prior to the making of the furvey—if fuch were ever made. But whether his lordfhip knew this or not, it is moft certain that his furveyors, in making plans and drawings of his eftate and the tenements upon it, would not introduce in the " margin " of their furvey" a houfe which, at leaft thirty-fix years previoufly, had been fold out of the Clopton family. When it is remembered who and what the " Poet " Jordan" was, and how ready he was to perpetrate any impofition upon the public, it feems moft probable that he invented the " margin of the furvey made by order "of Baron Carew," in order to impofe upon Malone, particularly as the exiftence of fuch such a survey or plan of a nobleman's estate was most likely to exist.

But was Malone imposed upon? Did he believe Jordan's statement, and regard the drawing as a genuine copy of an original representation of Shakespere's house?

Malone may have been predisposed to be deceived; he may have received the drawing with credence at first, as Walpole did Chatterton's records of ancient painters; but when Jordan got to improving the house, and adorning it with very probable coats-of-arms, it is hard to believe that Malone's faith was blind and unsuspecting; while it seems still harder to condemn him as *particeps criminis* in an attempt to pass off upon the public, as a "great" Gothic house of the time of Henry VII., renovated in the time of Queen Elizabeth (when houses were still built in exactly the same style and manner—the only difference being in the

New Place: *as it was reprefented by* Ireland.

(AN EXACT COPY OF THE ORIGINAL DRAWING.)

Face p. 47.

the " debafed" *details* of ornamentation, pinnacles, tracery, &c.), a drawing which only needs to be glanced at, and it is inftantly felf-condemned.

A fac-fimile of this drawing will be found in Knight's " Biography of Shakefpere" (note on New Place, p. 501). It has been repeatedly copied and prefented to the public, fo that it feems unneceffary to give it one more " laft appearance" in this place. It and the drawing given by Ireland may be called *arcades ambo*. The plate on the oppofite page, which accurately reproduces Ireland's, may fafely be regarded as twin-brother to the Jordan-Malone picture, the details being the fame in both, with the fingle variation already noticed. The barge-boards, as feen in the accompanying plate, which Ireland furbifhed up and added to the foiled impofition of Jordan, may well be compared to the fwaggering attempt of a gentleman,

out

out at elbows and deftitute of a change of linen, who feeks to impofe upon the public by mounting a clean collar on a manifeftly dirty fhirt.

The reader has only to examine and compare this picture with the picture of Ockwells to perceive, that though it might pafs mufter for the "oyfter-fhell" Gothic of Horace Walpole's fancy, it is as unlike the genuine domeftic architecture either of Henry VII.'s reign, or the "debafed" of Queen Elizabeth's, as Walpole's lath and plafter toy-fhop at Strawberry Hill was a baftard imitation of the ftyle he pretended to affect.* It will be obferved that the "timber and brick" defcribed

by

---

* The following letter, written by Horace Walpole, and now among the family papers of the Lord's Dacre, at Belhus, Effex, has never been made public. It has been kindly placed at the difpofal of the author by Sir Thomas Barrett Lennard, Bart., and will be read with intereft, both as difplaying the fycophantifh ftyle in which Walpole addreffed his fuperiors, and alfo his architectural tafte :—

["STRAWBERRY

by Dugdale have altogether vanished in Ireland's reprefentation, and that a flat, pafteboard-like uniformity of frontage is prefented, in every refpect oppofite to the character of true Gothic architecture, in which the lines are invariably broken up
by

"STRAWBERRY HILL, *July* 11*th*, 1777.

"I cannot receive joy from Bellhoufe, my dear Lord,
" without giving it, and without telling your Lordfhip
" how particularly kind I took it from Mr. Harding,
" in acquainting me with his intended marriage,—I had
" no right to expect fuch attention, but by my zealous
" wifhes for his happinefs. When anybody that is
" perfectly content, as he feems to be, thinks of making
" others happy, it is the beft proof of a good heart.
" When mifery is communicative, it may flow from
" want of pity, comfort, advice, or affiftance; but when
" happinefs is neither infolent nor felfifh, the monitor
" muft be benevolence. Without including myfelf in
" this defcription, I enjoy the fatisfaction your Lordfhip,
" Lady Dacre, Mrs. Harding, and Lord Camden muft
" have, in the felicity of fo deferving a young man.
" It is talking, too, like an old one, but furely all the
" rifing young men of the age have not Mr. Harding's
" good qualities. Your Lordfhip did me the honour
" of inviting me to Bellhoufe; it feemed ungrateful
" not to thank you, and yet gratitude was the true
" motive of my filence. I waited till I could tell you
" that I could accept the honour of your offer. I
" have had company, and various engagements that
" prevented me, and am not yet at liberty from the
" precarious

by gables, dormer windows, porches, and deep barge-boards, producing shadows, relief, and infinite variety. Ireland produced this wretched drawing in 1814. Mrs. Partheriche (concerning whom he was so ignorant that he could not spell her name correctly)* died in 1792. As the

---

"precarious state of H.R.H. the Duke of Gloucester's "health, and from expecting him and the Duchess in "England.[1]

"I was still more flattered, though very unworthy, "by your Lordship's thinking of consulting me on your "improvements at Bellhouse; nobody is more attached "to the beauty of your seat, nor shall see your additions "with more pleasure, but I have not the vanity to "presume to direct them. You have not only done "everything there with taste, my Lord, but to my taste "of 'ancienne noblesse;' and since cheesemongers can "be peers, I would have the mansions of old barons "powdered with quarterings for distinction; and since "Mr. Adams builds for so many of these, I wish he "would deviate from his style of Filigraine, and load "them with the Tuscan order, which admits very "speaking columns. "When

---

[1] His Royal Highness had married the Countess Waldegrave, daughter of Sir Edward Walpole, and niece to Horace Walpole.

---

* See quotation, p. 41.

Stratford-upon-Avon.

the fuppofed original picture was unfortunately deftroyed when in that lady's poffeffion, it might feem difficult for any ordinary mortal to make a copy of it in 1814: but difficulties of this fort are trifles eafily furmounted when genius, like another Jofhua, repeats the marvel of Ajalon, and puts back the courfes of time.*

Difmiffing both Jordan's invention and Ireland's impofition, there is another matter of error which deferves remark. Theobald afferts, that when Shakefpere
" repaired

"When I have a day at command, will Lady Dacre "and your Lordfhip allow me to make ufe of your "permiffion, and wait upon you. I will not take that "liberty, however, without afking if my vifit will be "feafonable. I am, my dear Lord, with the trueft "regards,
"Your Lordfhip's moft obt.
"humble fervant,
"HORACE WALPOLE."

---

* Appendix D.

"repaired and modelled" New Place, he gave it that name. This is not the fact. In the furvey of 1590 we find the following entry:—" Villielmus Underhill, "gen. tenet. libere quandam domum vo"catam *the Newe Place* cum pertinentiis "per reddit. per annum, xij*d*. fect. cur."

Conclufive evidence is thus afforded us, that years before the Poet had any intereft in the property, it was known by the name which has ever continued its "houfehold "words." Sir Hugh Clopton, who built the houfe of New Place, happens to have ftyled it in his will "the Great Houfe;" and fuch it has been fuppofed was its ordinary appellation. It is a fuppofition in fearch of a reafon. The phrafe feems rather an expreffion on the part of Sir Hugh, applied to his manfion as compared with the general fize and importance of the tenements that furrounded it, than the title of the place itfelf. It well deferved served the honourable designation; for when Queen Henrietta Maria, at the head of 3,000 foot, 1,500 horse, beside artillery and waggons, marched from Newark, in June, 1643 (on her progress to meet the king at Edge Hill, then proceeding to Oxford), and was met at Stratford by Prince Rupert, she was conducted to New Place as the most commodious residence fitted to receive her Majesty; and here she sojourned (as we are informed) "about three weeks."

Less direct, but important evidence of the "greatness" of New Place is afforded us by a consideration of the wealth and social position of Sir Hugh Clopton.

This Sir Hugh was a member of the ancient family of Clopton, of Clopton, in the parish of Stratford (Clopton House being about a mile out of Stratford). The family name was derived from the manor, which had been granted to the Cloptons

in

in the reign of Henry III., fo that Sir Hugh's anceftors had been men of rank and importance for at leaft two hundred and fifty years previous to his time. Sir Hugh became alderman of London, and ferved the office of Lord Mayor in the feventh year of the reign of Henry VII., 1492. His name ftill lives frefh and green in Stratford; for out of the abundance which he amaffed as a wool-ftapler in London, he not only adorned his native-place with the "Great Houfe," but he endeavoured to beautify the town itfelf, and alfo to benefit it by his charity. In the Guild Chapel of the Holy Crofs, adjoining New Place, there is a monument which was erected to his memory at the requeft of the Corporation of Stratford, by that Sir John Clopton, his defcendant, whofe marriage with Barbara Walker brought back New Place into the Clopton family.

The

The monument tells us of his " pious
" works, so many and so great, that they
" ought to be had in everlasting remem-
"brance, especially by this town and parish."

" He built ye stone bridge over Avon,
" with ye causey at ye west end; further
" manifesting his piety to God and love to
" this place of his nativity (as ye centurion
" in ye Gospel did to ye Jewish nation and
" religion by building them a synagogue),
" for at his sole charge this beautiful
" Chappel of ye Holy Trinity was rebuilt,
" temp. H. VII., and ye cross ile of ye
" Parish Church."

The inscription further relates his charities to the poor of Stratford and of
London:—£100 to poor housekeepers,
100 marks on their marriage to twenty
poor maidens, both in Stratford and London; making of bridges and highways;
founding exhibitions at Oxford and Cambridge; leaving money for poor prisoners,
money

money to hospitals, to the Mercers' Company, and "to ye parson of ye parish "where he lived" (a wholesome custom that has singularly fallen into desuetude). After all legacies and expenses are paid, he leaves the residue of his goods and chattels to "repairing decayed churches," "mending bridges and highways," "main-"taining poor children at school," and in portioning "honest maidens."

"This charitable Gent. died a Batcheler, "15th Sept., 1496, and was buried in St. "Margaret's Church, Lothbury."

The ancient and beautiful altar-tomb among the Clopton monuments in Stratford Church, without any effigy, but with quatrefoil panels, originally fitted with armorial bearings in brass, is most probably erected to his memory, because it stands on the precise spot where, according to his will, he directed that he should be buried, had he died at Stratford; and also

The Arms of London.   The Arms of *Sir Hugh Clopton, Knight.*   The Arms of the Merchants of the Staple.   The Arms of the Mercers' Company.

(The SHIELDS displayed upon the CANOPY of the ALTAR-TOMB in the CLOPTON CHAPEL, STRATFORD-UPON-AVON.)

Face p. 57.

alfo becaufe the arms carved in the arch above it are thofe of Sir Hugh, difplayed with the arms of the Corporation of London, of which he was Lord Mayor, of the Mercers' Company, and of the Wool Staplers, to all which bodies he belonged.

In corroboration of this probability, which might be pretty fafely afferted as fact, any vifitor to the Guild Chapel may obferve on the face of the porch-way, over the arch, a feries of fhields, in receffes. It has been already fhown that this portion of Holy Crofs—the nave and porch—were rebuilt by Sir Hugh Clopton. Accordingly, among the fhields we find, fimilar to the fhields over the monument in the church, the arms of the City of London, the arms of the Wool Staplers, and the arms of Clopton, *quartered with Cockfield* (Clopton quartering, a Crofs patèe, fitchée in the foot; Cockfield, a lion rampant).*

The

---
* Appendix E.

The quarterings agreeing precisely with the display in the "Visitation of Warwick-shire," and therefore somewhat strengthening the assertion of the "Visitation," that the Cloptons and the Cockfields were *temp.* Edward I. two distinct families, and not that Walter de Cockfield was a Clopton, who assumed the surname of Cockfield, which name continued in use down to the time of Sir Hugh Clopton's grandfather, *temp.* Richard II., after which it disappeared, and Clopton only was used.

In his Survey of London and Westminster (under the title "Mercers"), Stowe alludes to Sir Hugh, as follows:—

" Sir Hugh Clopton, all his lifetime a
" Bathchelaur, Maior, 1492, buried at St.
" Margaret's in Lothbury, 1496. He
" dwelt in Lothbury, where long after
" was the sign of the *Wind-Mill;* and
" where Sir Robert Large, sometime
" Lord

"Lord Maior, had lived before.* This man was born at Clopton, in Warwickshire, a mile from Stratford-upon-Avon, where he builded a fair stone bridge of eighteen arches, and glazed the chancel windows"

---

* This Sir Robert Large (Lord Mayor of London in 1439, died 1441), was the Mercer to whom Caxton was apprenticed when he came to London from the Weald of Kent. Stowe shows us that Caxton and Sir Hugh both lived in the same house in Lothbury, and we know they were both members of the Company of Mercers. When we remember that Caxton went over to Ghent and Bruges in the interest of the Mercers' Company, when the wool trade was suffering through the quarrel between England and Philip the Good of Burgundy, and that Sir Hugh Clopton was not only the successor of Sir Robert Large in his house and place of business, but also a distinguished member of the Company of Mercers, it seems almost a certainty that Caxton and Sir Hugh must have been well known to one another; and it is possible, perhaps probable, that by Sir Hugh the first books printed in England, "The Game of Chess," published 1474, the "Poems of Chaucer," "Æsop's Fables," "Reynard the Fox," and others, would be taken down to his Great House in Stratford, where the wonder and admiration of his neighbours would make the walls echo with the name of Caxton, the introducer of the invention which, in little more than a century later, was to carry forth from that same house the immortal thoughts of him, whose words, winged by Caxton's aid, have flown from pole to pole.

"windows of the fame Parifh Church "where his arms did ftand. Which, "as William Smith, fometime Rouge "Dragon, hath obferved, differed much "from the coat fet up for him, painted "in a target, in the Mercers' Hall, "which indeed was the arms of the "Cloptons of Suffolk."

Thefe facts prefent to the mind one of England's worthies, a true Chriftian gentleman in the fulleft and beft fenfe of the phrafe. It is a matter of furprife that a man of fuch excellent parts and character, and fo intimately connected with the houfe and place where Shakefpere lived, fhould be fo much overlooked, as he is, by writers upon Stratford and its antiquities.

It is not, however, upon his genuine nobility of character that we have here to dwell; but upon his tafte, his love for art, and his delight in architecture. It is fomething more than a fanciful
idea

idea for us to believe that the taſte of Sir Hugh Clopton influenced the mind of Shakeſpere. Inſtead of a fancy, this ſeems to be a faƈt. The "New "Place," which he ereƈted, was deſtroyed ſomewhere about 1720, and no repreſentation of it remains to portray it to us; but one piece of building, within a dozen yards of the ſpot where it ſtood, is indicative of Sir Hugh's taſte. The nave of the Guild Chapel was rebuilt by him, at preciſely the ſame period that Dean Balſhall (then Vicar of Stratford), was rebuilding the chancel of the Pariſh Church, to which it is clear that Sir Hugh generouſly contributed. Stowe informs us that the perpendicular tracery of the windows in this chancel was filled with ſtained glaſs, at the expenſe of Sir Hugh Clopton, whoſe arms Dugdale ſaw emblazoned upon the glaſs. There can be no difficulty
in

in conjecturing what sort of residence "New Place" must have been—how architecturally correct—how excellent in proportion—how artistic in design—how pure in the style and detail of its ornamentation—how deserving of its master's designating it the "Great House" of Stratford, when we refer to his will, and compare its special provisions for the repairing of churches, the building of bridges, the construction of highways, with the work that he did himself accomplish in erecting Stratford Bridge, building the nave of the Holy Cross Chapel, and aiding in the erection of the chancel of the Parish Church. Those portions of the Stratford churches, in which Sir Hugh was interested, are, even amidst the lavish richness of ecclesiastical architecture in Warwickshire, justly reckoned superb specimens of the Perpendicular period.

Of "New Place" Shakespere became
the

the lord and mafter in 1597. The houfe was then rather more than one hundred years old. It would need to be "repaired and modelled," particularly as it had belonged to three refpective families within the half century before Shakefpere purchafed it, and had paffed out of the Clopton family about a year prior to his birth. Of the repairs that he made, we know nothing; but it is eafy to underftand how much his mind may have been impreffed with the ftately beauty of New Place from his earlieft childhood. No inhabitant of Stratford, feeing Sir Hugh's "Great Houfe" and the church that he alfo rebuilt alongfide it, could fail to know them and to admire them, much lefs a boy of Shakefpere's obfervation and appreciative mind. New Place adjoins the Guild Chapel and the Grammar School. There the boy was taught; and day by day, as he went

bounding

bounding forth from school, the firſt object that met his view was Sir Hugh's houſe, next the church. While yet a child of between three and four years of age, a ſale took place. He may, on the very day of the ſale, have been holding to his nurſe's ſide, and making his earlieſt obſervations upon men and things, as he paſſed the chapel of Holy Croſs, and have ſeen the family of Underhill arrive to acquire poſſeſſion of "New Place." All this is perfectly poſſible; and if this or anything ſimilar occurred, it might impreſs upon the boy's thoughts that New Place *had been ſold!* Might it not again? Who can tell, whether in his early days the boy Shakeſpere's mind had not been taught by old Sir Hugh's taſte to appreciate and admire the beautiful in art; had not been fired with ambition to go to London, as Sir Hugh (the pride of Stratford, and its benefactor) had done, and

and by dint of labour and perseverance to make an independence, and return like him to Stratford, and live honoured and beloved among the townsfolk of his native place? Who can tell whether this same boy may not often and often have stood ruminating under the shadows of the buttresses of Holy Cross, admiringly examining the gables and casements, the porch and antique barge-boards of the " great house," and resolving, should any sale take place there again, if he were a man and had the means, it should have but one master—one, himself possessed of tastes like Sir Hugh's, who would " repair " and preserve the ancestral mansion?

In any biographies of Shakespere or histories of Stratford which may have been written heretofore, New Place has been

been little more than mentioned. A house was built upon it at such a date, sold at another, purchased by Shakespere at another, and in it he died. No one has ever as yet opened the pages of ancient records to tell us much more about it than that it belonged to the Clopton family, and was built by Sir Hugh Clopton.

The time has perhaps come when it is desirable that the public should become possessed of more particulars concerning it; in fact, when every available information should be produced to relate its history.

That it was Shakespere's dwelling-place is the cause of its interest in public esteem; but that interest will be in no degree decreased if we know something about the associations of the place, and of the family to which it chiefly belonged, especially as that family must have been
well

well known to Shakefpere; and members of it, that were his contemporaries, play no obfcure part in the hiftory of his times. Whoever he may be that undertakes to give the world a true and fufficient account of New Place muft inform his readers concerning the Cloptons of Clopton Houfe, fince the hiftory of New Place and its varied fortunes is as clofely twined around the Clopton ftem as the ivy around the oak.

On the oppofite page will be found a pedigree fet forth, which has appeared abfolutely effential to the accomplifhment of the author's purpofe. By reference to it the reader will be able to follow him much more eafily; and in order to fecure perfpicuity—as the fame names are repeated in feveral defcents—thofe have been alphabetically labelled to which it feems neceffary to direct particular attention.

It

It has been shown (p. 16), that New Place was built in the reign of Henry VII., not later than 1490, by Sir Hugh Clopton, formerly Lord Mayor of London (pedigree AA). Sir Hugh was a younger son of John Clopton, of Clopton — *temp.* Henry VI.,—and being a younger son, both he and his brother John fought their fortunes as merchants of the Staple, in London. Dying a bachelor, Sir Hugh bequeathed his residence of New Place to his elder brother's grandson and heir, William Clopton (AB), in whom accordingly both Clopton House and New Place became vested.

The will of Sir Hugh Clopton, bearing date 14th Sept., 1496, was proved at Lambeth on the 4th day of October in the same year. He describes himself therein as " citezein, mercer, and alderman of London," and desires that if he die in London, or within twenty miles thereof,

thereof, he fhould be buried in the church of St. Margaret's, Lothbury; but if at Stratford-upon-Avon, to be buried in the parifh church there, within the chapel of our Lady, between the altar of the fame and the chapel of the Trinity next adjoining, his body to be brought to ground with four torches and four tapers, and no more.

After detailing an agreement with one Dowland and divers other mafons about the building of the chapel of the Trinity, and the tower of a fteeple to the fame, and mentioning his father and mother by name (John and Agnes), there is a difpofition of fundry legacies to charitable and religious ufes to confiderable length; after which bequefts to divers individuals; and, finally, entries relative to the devife of his property, in thefe words :—

Item.

Item.—I will as for my landes and rentes all such is of copy holde that Thomas Clopton the yonger and I be feoffed in remayne holy to hym and to his heires after my decesse for ever and for lak of issue to the right heires of the lordship of Clopton *And to William Clopton I bequeith my great house in Stratford upon Avon and all other my lands and tenements beinge in Wilmecote in the Brigge towne and Stratford with reversion and services and duetes thereunto belonginge remayne to my cousin Wm. Clopton* and for lak of issue of hym to remayne to the right heires of the lordship of Clopton for ever being heires males   Also I will that CC marc that Doctor Balsale delyvered me be by the advise and discrecion of my executours employed to the use behoofe and moost profitte of the college of Stratford-upon-Avon by the consent and advice of the wardeyn with other sadde prestis and honest men of the towne   And all such housing and tenementes as I have within the towne of Caleys I will remayn to my cousin Hugh Clopton the elder and also the reversion of the house that I dwell in att London and the termes of the same.

By the *inquiſition poſt mortem* upon *Sir Hugh Clopton*, it appears that he died feised of the following property in Stratford :—

De

Stratford-upon-Avon. 71

De uno burgagio jacente in *Chapell strete* in Stretford predicta ex oposito capelle ex parte boriali et de uno dimidio burgagio jacente in *Ely strete* alias dicta *Swynne strete* et de uno burgagio in *High strete* et de uno orreo et gardino jacente in *Henley strete* et de uno dimidio burgagio jacente in *Church strete* in Stretford predicta et de duobus toftis quatuor virgatis terre quatuor acris prati et viginti acris pasture cum pertinentijs in *Bryggetowne* in parochia de Stretford Et quod idem Hugo ante obitum suum fuit seisitus in dominico suo ut de feodo de uno tenemento jacente in Stratford predicta in *Rother strete* vocato *Balsals place* et de uno gardino jacente in *Church strete* et de uno tenemento jacente in *High strete* super corneram de le Corne market in quo Johannes Balamy inhabitat et de aleo tenemento in *Chapel strete* buttante super le Corne market in quo Wolfridus Smyth inhabitat in Stretford predicta.*

Thefe documents will fhow that William Clopton (AB), who had inherited the Clopton eftates in 1486, received a very

---

* According to this will, it appears that all this property here recited was demifed and let to Roger Paget and Elizabeth his wife, for term of life of the faid Roger.

very considerable addition to his patrimony by the death—ten years later—of his great uncle, in 1496.

But, together with this accession, he found himself master of two considerable mansions, removed little more than a mile from one another; viz., Clopton House adjoining the town, and New Place within it.

Whether this gentleman kept up both the houses there is no evidence to show; but as we have proof of New Place being let by his son (B), it seems probable that William Clopton (AB) contented himself with the patrimonial residence of Clopton, and set the example which his son followed. Having enjoyed his estate for twenty-five years, he died in 1521, little more being known of him than that for some offence to the Crown he received a pardon from Henry VIII.

By the *inquisition post mortem*, it appears

pears that he was feifed of the following property in Stratford, and retained poffeffion of New Place:—

In uno burgagio jacente in strata vocata *Chapel strete* in Stretford super Aven ex parte boriali capelle Sancte Trinitatis in Stratford predicta in comitatu predicto et de uno burgagio jacente in *Chapel strete* predicta uno capite inde abuttante versus Hugonem Raynold ex parte Australi et alio capite inde abuttante versus quandam stratam vocatam *Shepe strete* ex parte Boriali et de uno burgagio jacente in strata vocata *High strete* in Stratford predicta uno capite abuttante versus fundum Magistri Gilde Sancte Trinitatis de Stratford ex parte Boriali et alio capite inde abuttante versus stratam vocatam *Slystrete* ex parte Australi ac de uno burgagio jacente in strata vocata *High strete* in Stretford predicta uno capite inde abuttante versus tenementum Magistri Gilde Sancte Trinitatis predicte ex parte Australi et alio capite inde abuttante versus Willielmum Staffordshire ex parte Boriali Necnon de uno Burgagio jacente in strata vocata *Briggestrete* in Stratford predicta ac eciam de quodam orreo jacente in strata vocata *Henley strete* in Stratford predicta ac de quodam shopa jacente in strata vocata *Wode strete* quam Robertus Gonyatt modo tenet et occupat et de uno burgagio
jacente

jacente in strata vocata *Rother market* in Stretford predicta in quo Deonisia Aylys vidua modo inhabitat ac de uno burgagio jacente in strata vocata *Grenhul strete* in Stretford predicta in quo Nicholaus Norres modo inhabitat necnon de uno burgagio jacente in strata vocata *Church strete* in Stretford predicta &c Necnon de alio burgagio jacente in *Church strete* in Stratford predicta in quo Johannes Ashurste modo inhabitat uno capite inde abuttante versus Episcopum Wigornensis ex parte Occidentali et alio capite inde abuttante versus vicum Regis vocatum *Church strete* ac de duobus gardinis in Stretford predicta abuttantibus versus Johem Hubandys ex parte Boriali et versus dictum Magistrum Gilde predicte ex parte Australi necnon de dimidio burgagio jacente in *Elystrete* in Stratford predicta nunc dimisso et locato pro quodam orreo.

The above William (AB) was succeeded by his son, bearing the same name (B), who lived in possession of the combined estates from 1521 to 1560, at which latter date he died. His will is dated January 4th, and we learn from the inquisition that he expired on the same day at Clopton. The death of this William

Clopton (B) brings to light the firft fact explanatory of the caufes which led to New Place fubfequently becoming the property of Shakefpere. The will bears the name of " William Bott," one of the attefting witneffes. There are traces of Botts in the regifter of Stratford, though the author has vainly fearched for fome mention of this perfon, whofe name is on record as one of the practifing folicitors of Stratford at the period.

June 2, 1575.—William, sonne of Robt. Bott (buried).
September 2, 1576.—Sonne to Edward Botte.
July 18, 1588.—Margery, daughter of Ralph Bott, deceased.
January 19, 1591.—Anne Botte, deceased.

The probability is that the Botts were only profeffionally connected with Stratford, and belonged to fome outlying parifh or hamlet. However this may be, it is certain that William Bott was a lawyer

lawyer in practice at Stratford,* and that he was profeſſionally engaged by William Clopton of Clopton (B).

After his death, the inquiſition was taken on the 17th day of June, 2nd of Elizabeth (1560), at Warwyck, and the Jurors found that he died ſeiſed (inter alia) in his demeſne as of fee—

De et in uno tenemento sive burgagio cum pertinentijs in Stratford super Aven in dicto comitatu Warr̃ in vico ibidem vocato la Chappell strete modo in tenura sive occupacione Willielmi Bott.

The ſame inquiſition informs us, that the ſon and heir William Clopton (C) was at that date "twenty-two years of age."

In due courſe of years this William (C)

---

* Attorneys of Stratford about that date :—Mr. Thomas Truſſell, Mr. William Court, Mr. Edward Davies, Mr. William Bott, Mr. Richard Spooner, Mr. Richard Symmons.

(C) came alfo to die, as the pedigree fhows, in the year 1592.

The Book of Adminiftrations, in an entry regarding the goods of this gentleman, reveals to us not only the bufinefs, but alfo the blood relationfhip between the Cloptons and the Botts; and thus we receive a complete infight into a tranfaction that feems fingular, regarding which no previous writer has given us any information.

The following extract is moft important:—

Octobris, 1597.

WILLIELMUS CLOPTON.

Administratio Comissa antea, mense Maij, 1592.

Duodecimo die emanavit commissio *Johanni Bott,* PROXIMO CONSANGUINEO *Willielmi Clopton,* nuper dum vixit de Clopton, in comitatu Warwici, defuncti, habentis, &c., ad administrandum bona, jura, et credita ejusdem, per *Annam Clopton,* ejus relictam, jam defunctam, non administrata,

Blasij Johannis, 1603.

Johannis, 1605.

administrata, de bene, &c., in persona Thome White, notarij publici, procuratoris, legitime constituti, jurate.

Blasij, 1605.

In what way John Bott happened to be "proximo confanguineo" to William Clopton the author muft confefs his profound ignorance; for Heralds' College can give him no relief. No doubt there has been an omiffion in the pedigree, wherever the link between the Botts and Cloptons occurred; but the above extract places it beyond all queftion that, in October, 1597, one John Bott, as the neareft of kin in the male line, after the death of Miftrefs Anne Clopton in 1596, the widow of William, adminiftered the eftate, it is to be prefumed, as the friend and relative of the Countefs of Totnefs, and Anne Clopton, of Sledwick, her fifter, the co-heireffes of the late William Clopton (C).

What

Stratford-upon-Avon.

What the connection between John Bott and William Bott was, the author has not discovered. They were probably father and son, or brothers—the latter being the more probable of the two conjectures. That they were close blood relatives is beyond a doubt.

Having dug up these facts, it will not surprise the most ordinary mind to find that William Bott, of Stratford-upon-Avon, solicitor, tenant of New Place, relative, and family lawyer to the Cloptons—witness to the will of a father, and adviser to his successor, aged twenty-two —took an early opportunity of improving upon the chances which fortune had cast in his way.

William Clopton (B) died 1560.

William Clopton, the administration of whose estate subsequently in 1597 is referred to above, (C) succeeded, and in 1563 he was induced to sell New Place to his

his late father's tenant, lawyer, and his own blood relative.

The tranſactions between Bott and William Clopton were conſiderable, for by the indenture which follows it will be ſeen that Bott had a knack of gaining poſſeſſion of land belonging to the Clopton eſtate.

Indentur̃ inŕ Willm̃ Clopton et Willm̃ Bott.

𝕮𝖍𝖎𝖘 𝕴𝖓𝖉𝖊𝖓𝖙𝖚𝖗𝖊 made the xth daye of Januarye in the syxte yere of the reigne of our soúaigne ladye Elizabeth by the grace of God quene of England Fraunce and Irelande defendor of the faith &c betwene Willm̃ Clopton of Clopton in the countye of Warr̃ Esquyer on the one partye and Willm̃ Bott of Stratforde uppon Avon in the said Countye gentleman on the other partye wytnesseth that the said Willm̃ Clopton for and in consederacõn of and for dyúse som̃es of money to hym in hande att and before the ensealinge hereof whereof and wherewyth the said Willm̃ Clopton doth acknowledge hym selfe thereof well and trulye satysfyed contented and paid and the said Willm̃ Bott his heires executors and administrators thereof clerely acquyted exoñated and dyschardged

chardged by these p̃ntes hath gyven and graunted
bargayned and solde and by these p̃sentes doth
clerelye and frelye gyve graunte bargayne and
sell to the said Willm̃ Bott all those his three
pastures of grounde called the nether Ingon alias
Ington and all that his meadowe called Synder
meadowe lyinge and beinge in nether Ingon alias
Ington in the paryshe of Bisshopps Hampton in
the said Countye of Warr̃ nowe or late in the
tenure or occupac̃on of Rycharde Charnocke and
Willm̃ Baylyes of Welon and the assignes of the
said Rycharde Charnocke and all that his wyndemyll foure yardes of errable land and twentye and
nyne leyes scituate lyinge and beynge in the
Feildes of olde Stratforde and in the home nexte
adioyninge to the said feildes and all that his
meadowe lyinge in Shotterye meydowe nowe or
late in the occupac̃on of John Combes and John
Lewys alias Atkyns To have and to holde the
said pastures meadowes wyndemylles lande and
leys and all and singuler there apptenaunces to
the said Willm̃ Bott his heires and assignes for
eumore to the onlye use and behoufe of the said
Willm̃ Bott his heires and assignes for ever And
also the said Willm̃ Clopton hath bargayned &
solde by these p̃sentes all and all maner of evidences deedes wrytinges cħers and mynymentes
that be touchynge and concnynge onlye the
p̃misses or any parte or parcell of them and the
said evidences dedes wrytinges cħers and mynymentes the said Willm̃ Clopton couenaunteth and
                                    graunteth

graunteth by these p̃sentes to and wyth the said
Willm̃ Bott his executors or assignes to delyuer
or cause to be delyu�footed to hym the said Willm̃
Bott his executors or assignes before the feaste of
Easter next ensuinge the date herecf and fyr-
thermore the said Willm̃ Clopton for him his
heires executors and administrators couenaunteth
and graunteth by these p̃sentes to and wyth the
said Willm̃ Bott that he the said Willm̃ Clopton
shall before the feaste of Easter make or cause to
be made to the said Willm̃ Bott his heires or assignes a good suer suffycyente laufull and indefy-
cyble estate in the lawe in fee symple of and in
the said pastures meadowes leyes of pasture
wyndemyll and errable lande wyth all and singuler there app̃tenaunces be yt by fyne feoffament
dede or dedes inrolled release confirmac̃on re-
couỹe wyth voucher or vouchers wyth warrantye
agaynste all men or wyth out warrantye as cane
and shalbe deuysed or aduised by the learned
councell of the said Willm̃ Bott his heires or assignes and furthermore the said Willm̃ Clopton
for hym his heires executors and administrators
couenaunteth and graunteth by these p̃sentes to
and wyth the said Willm̃ Bott his executors and
administrators that the said pastures meadowe
wyndemyll and errable lande att the daye of the
date hereof be clerelye dyscharged of all and from
all former bargaynes sales dowres ioyntors leases
statutes m̃chaunte and of the staple Recognisances
iudgementes fynes am̃cyamentes condempnac̃ons
and

and all other chardges and incomberances whatsoever they be the rentes and ꝯuices to the cheife
lorde or lordes of the fee from hensforth dewe
and accustomed to be paide onlye excepted and
also the said Willm̄ Clopton for hym his heires
executors and administrators couenaunteth and
graunteth by these p̄sentes to and wyth the said
Willm̄ Bott his heires executors and administrators that he the said Willm̄ Clopton and Anne
his wyffe shall before the fourthe daye of Maye
nexte ensuinge the date hereof knowledge a fyne
before one of the quenes maiestyes iustyces of the
Kinges benche or comon place to be levyed before the Quenes Justices at Westm̄ of and for the
said pastures meadowe wyndemyll leyes of pasture and errable lande wyth all and singuler there
apꝑtenaunces and also the said Willm̄ Clopton for
hym his heires executors and administrators coue-
nuanteth and graunteth by these presentes to and
wyth the said Willm̄ Bott his heires executors and
assignes that he the said Willm̄ Clopton and his
heires shall att all tymes hereafter and from tyme
to tyme when and as often as he or they shalbe
thereunto reasonablye required by the said Willm̄
Bott his heires or assignes doo suffer and cause
to be done and suffered all and eūy suche further
acte and actes thinge and thinges as shalbe reasonablye required by the learned councell of the
said Willm̄ Bott his heires or assignes for the further assurance and suer makinge of the premisses
to the said Willm̄ Bott his heires or assignes for
euermore

euermore In wytnesse whereof eyther party to these p̃sente Indentures intc̃haungeably have putto there seales the daye and yere firste above wrytten Et memorand̃ qd̃ t̃cio die Aprilis anno Sup̃script̃ p̃dcũs Wills̃ Clopton venit coram dc̃a dña Regina in Cancellar̃ sua apud Westm̃ et recognouit Indentur̃ p̃dcãm et oñia et singula in eadem content̃ et sp̃ificat̃ in forma sup̃dict̃.

January, in the 6th of Eliz., would be 1563-4—three months before Shakeſpere was born. Upon the authority of Wheler, the author has aſſumed that the ſale of New Place occurred the year previous (1563). Wheler is commonly moſt accurate, and the above ſale gives weight to his aſſertion, becauſe it proves that Bott was at that time making purchaſes from William Clopton. The *Fines* of 1563 are ſilent, though it muſt be obſerved that there is a total abſence of all *Fines* in the Record Office for Michaelmas Term of that year ; which is to be accounted for by the faƈt that the plague was raging

raging. It is moſt probable that the ſale took place at that time; and that the late Mr. Wheler had met with ſome private trace of it for which the author has fruitleſſly ſearched among public papers.

That William Bott purchaſed New Place upon ſpeculation appears moſt probable, becauſe it only remained in his poſſeſſion for the period of four years. The *Fines*, Michaelmas Term, 9th Eliz., ſhow us that the ſale by Bott to Underhill took place at that date.

Warr̃ 1567.

Hec est finalis concordia fc̃a in Cur̃ Dñe Regine apud Westm̃ in crastino Sc̃i Martini anno regnor̃ Elizabeth dei grã Angł Franc̃ et Hiƀnie Regine fidei defensoris &c a conqũ nono coram Jacobo Dyer Ric̃o Weston Joh̃e Walshe & Ric̃o Harpur Justic̃ et alijs dñe Regine fidelib3 tunc ibi p̃sentib3 inr̃ Willm̃ Underehyll quer̃ et Willm̃ Botte et Elizabeth ux̃em eius et Albanũ Hetoñ deforc̃ de uno mesuagio et uno gardino cum p̃tiñ in Stretford sup̃ Aven unde p̃litum convenc̃ois sũm
fuit

fuit int̃ eos in eadm̃ Cur scilt̃ qd̃ p̃dc̃i Willm̃s Botte et Elizabeth et Albanus recogñ p̃dc̃t teñ cum ptiñ esse jus ip̃ius Willm̃i Underehyll ut iħ que idem Willm̃s ħet de dono p̃dc̃oȓ Willm̃i Botte et Elizabeth et Albani Et iħ remiseȓ et quiet᷉ clam̃ de ip̃is Willm̃o Botte et Elizabeth et Albano et hered̃ suis p̃dc̃õ Willm̃o Underehyll et hered̃ suis impp̃m Et p̃terea idem Willm̃s Botte concessit p̃ se et hered̃ suis q̃d ip̃i warant᷉ p̃dc̃o Willm̃o Underehyll et hered̃ suis p̃dict᷉ teñ cum ptiñ cont᷉a p̃dc̃m Willm̃ Botte et hered̃ suos impp̃m Et ult᷉ius idem Albanus concessit p̃ se et hered̃ suis q̃d ip̃i warant᷉ p̃dc̃o Willm̃o Underehyll et hered̃ suis p̃dict teñ cum ptiñ cont᷉a p̃dc̃m Albanũ et hered̃ suos impp̃m Et insup ijdem Willm̃s Botte et Elizabeth concesseȓ p̃ se et hered̃ ip̃ius Elizabeth q̃d ip̃i warant᷉ p̃dc̃o Willm̃o Underehyll et hered̃ suis p̃dc̃a teñ cum ptiñ cont᷉a p̃dc̃am Elizabeth et hered̃ suos impp̃m Et p̃ hac recogñ remissione quietaclam̃ warant᷉ fine et concordia idem Willm̃s Underehyll dedit p̃dc̃is Willm̃o Botte et Elizabeth et Albano quadraginta libras sterlingoȓ.

[Endorsed are the proclamations secundum formam statuti.]

By this ſale New Place was reſcued from the hands of a graſping lawyer, and paſſed into the poſſeſſion of a family long connected

connected with Eatington, and Idlicote, near Shipston-upon-Stour. The Underhills, as the abstract of pedigree herewith given shows, were originally a Staffordshire family, and settled at Eatington, a few miles from Stratford, on property belonging to the Shirleys.* The younger son of Edward Underhill purchased the estate of Idlicote, a short distance from Eatington, in the 10th year of the reign of Elizabeth (1568), from Ludovic Greville, and so established the junior branch of the Underhills as a family in Warwickshire. This William (marked A on the pedigree) had a son, also named William (marked B), who married his first cousin, Mary, of Eatington. His sons, Sir Hercules and William, were staunch and loyal supporters of the cause of Charles I., and were compelled to redeem

---

* Appendix F.

redeem their estate from the Republicans for £1,177 8s. 6d.

William Underhill (B) was the person by whom the purchase of New Place was made. By referring to the will of his father (in the Appendix G) it is evident that the Underhills possessed property in Stratford-upon-Avon; and therefore the purchase of New Place by William Underhill is readily understood. His name is repeatedly found among the fines levied about the years 1570 to 1590,* proving that he was anxious to accumulate as much landed property as he could in the neighbourhood of Stratford-upon-Avon; in fact, that he was ambitious to establish the younger branch of the Underhills at Idlicote in as great affluence as the senior branch at Eatington. It was an ambition destined

---

* Appendix G.

destined to be disappointed in the person of his grandson (C), who having married Alice, the daughter of Sir Thomas Lucy, of Charlecote, had the misfortune to become a widower, and then to become enamoured of a widow, the relict of one Van Bommel, a rich Dutch merchant in London. This lady estranged Sir William from rural life, led him to London, and drew him into commercial speculation. He embarked in the gunpowder trade; the mills were blown up, and the property blown to the winds at the same time. His son, Hercules (D), was involved, along with his father, and the result was, that in 1754 the estate was sold to the Hon. Heneage Legge, by the grandson Samuel (E), whose sister Alice (F) was allied with the family of the Lucys of Charlecote, having married the Rev. George Hammond, Rector of Hampton Lucy, who succeeded his uncle, William Lucy

Lucy, D.D., in the rectory, 1724. A monument to the memory of Mr. Hammond, and Alice Underhill, his wife, may be seen in the vestry of the modernly rebuilt church of Hampton Lucy; the apsidal east end of which, lately added by the present owner of Charlecote, aided by the genius of Mr. Gilbert Scott, has transformed this church into a sort of small cathedral; and, in the midst of the beauties and associations of Hampton Lucy and Charlecote, has furnished the lovers of architecture with a central object upon which the eye rests with gratitude to the liberality and taste of the present master of Charlecote.

From 1567 to 1597 William Underhill continued the proprietor of New Place.* It is vain at this remote date to speculate upon the causes which led to Shakespere's

---

* Appendix H.

Shakefpere's purchafe of New Place. Certainly there was no neceffity for William Underhill to fell any portion of his property. On the contrary, we have the beft proof that he had the defire and ability to increafe his landed eftate; and we can eftimate its value when we recall the fact before ftated, that his fon, Sir Hercules, during the Civil War was glad to compound for it, by paying down £1,177. There is one fact concerning the fale of New Place which is worth noting. It was fold to Shakefpere in the Eafter Term of 1597; and Underhill was himfelf dead and buried July 13th of the fame year.

This fact rather favours the idea that New Place was fold from fome private or perfonal motive to Shakefpere; for it moft certainly was not fold as a bufinefs tranfaction. William Underhill is known to us as an accumulator of landed property

perty, not as a man who had any necesfity to part with a single acre of his estate. It is probable that Shakespere was acquainted with the Underhills, and it may be that William Underhill was aware of the Poet's desire to possess himself of the property at New Place. New Place would not be a residence at which Fulk, or Hercules—the future Sir Hercules, Royalist, and favourite of King Charles—would be ever likely to reside, particularly as Idlicote itself was so contiguous to Stratford. It will be seen by the pedigree that Fulk died the year after his father, and the inheritance passed to his brother Hercules, a minor. Had Fulk Underhill died the year before his father's death, a reason for the sale of New Place would have been supplied us. As it is, the probabilities are strongly in favour of the belief that Shakespere was personally intimate with the Underhill family

family; and both Fulk and Hercules, youths of about seventeen and nineteen years of age, were poffibly anxious that before their father died, the Poet and actor fhould be gratified in his wifh, and New Place fecured to him. The facts, however, are thefe: in Eafter Term, 1597, the fale was effected, and on the 13th of July, William Underhill was buried. The preceding documents the author believes have never before been publifhed; the following was difcovered by Mr. Halliwell:—

Pasch. 39 Eliz.

Inter Willielmum Shakespeare quer̃ et Willielmum Underhill, generosum deforc̃, de uno mesuagio, duobus horreis, et duobus gardinis, cum pertinentijs, in Stratford super Avon, unde placitum convencionis sum̃, fuit inter eos, &c. scilicet quod predictus Willielimus Underhill recogñ, predicta tenementa cum pertinentijs esse jus ipsius Willielmi´ Shakespeare ut illa que idem Willielmus habet de dono predicti Willielmus Underhill, et ilt remisit et quietclam̃ de se et
hered̃

hered suis predicto Willielmo Shakespeare et hered suis in perpetuum; et preterea idem Willielmus Underhill concessit pro se et hered suis quod ipsi warant predicto Willielmo Shakespeare et hered suis predicta tenementa cum pertinentijs in perpetuum. Et pro hac &c. idem Willielmus Shakespeare dedit predicto Willielmo Underhill sexaginta libras sterlingorum.

In glancing over thefe dry legal papers, unearthed from the charnel-houfe of hiftory, we are brought into contact with the acts of men, whofe lives would be unknown had they not been preferved from oblivion by the embalming law. Shakefpere's acquaintances, neighbours, perhaps friends, are brought before us in fuch documents, and in the regifters of parifh churches. Thefe, and their tombftones, are almoft our only fources of information concerning the men and women who were of note and confequence in and about Stratford, who muft have been familiar with the Poet, and
who

who might, by the labour of a few hours, have left us records of him which would have made the world grateful through all its hours to come.

Let us be thankful, however, for poffeffing records that do furvive the deftruction of time; and accepting them, if we cannot re-people the paft, at leaft we can catch a glimpfe here and there of forms familiar to the Poet both before and during his New Place life.

Among the Special Commiffions taken for the county of Warwick, now preferved in the Record Office, is an inquifition upon the eftate of Ambrofe, Earl of Warwick, dated 32 Eliz. (1591). The document is very lengthy, and one of very great intereft. Some years back, attention was drawn to it by Mr. Cole, but as yet no antiquary has been found having a publifher of fufficient fpirit to rifk its publication.
The

The following epitome of such portions as serve the object of the author will be read with interest. Among the commissioners will be observed the name of Charles Hales, to which the attention of the reader is especially directed, for reasons which will appear hereafter.

Special Commissions (Co. Warwick) *temp*. Eliz.

Inquisitio capta apud Warwic⁹ et Stratford super Avon sexto die Octobris anno regni domine nostre Elizabethe Dei Gracia Anglie Francie et Hibernie Regine fidei defensoris &c tricesimo secundo coram Fulcone Grevile milite Thoma Leygh milite Johanne Puckeringe armigeris servientibus dicte domine Regine ad legem, Thome Dabridgcourt armigero, et Carolo Hales armigero, virtute Comissionis dicte domine Regine extra Scaccarium nobis et alijs directe ad inquirendum et supervidendum de omnibus et singulis manerijs terris tenementis et hereditamentis in comitate predicto nuper Ambrosij comitis Warwicensis Et de quibusdam articulis eidem Comissioni annexis per sacramentum Johis Turner generosi Richardi Woodward generosi Radulphi Townesend generosi Johannis Fulwood generosi Humfridi Brace Radulphi Lorde Willielmi Wyatt Johannis Sadler
Ricardi

Stratford-upon-Avon.

Ricardi Walford Georgij Frauncis Thome Nosor Willielmi Harbage Georgij Gybbes Willielmi Taylor Thome Warde Johannis Collins THOME SHACKESPERE Johannis Barrett Thome Goddard Richardi Masters Willielmi Lapworth Thome Preyst Ricardi Williams et Roberti Farefax qui dicunt ut sequitur

* * * *

MANERIUM DE NOVO STRATFORD

Burgus sive villa de Stratford super Avon cum membris in comitatu Warr^9.

* * * *

Smythe strete

THOMAS SHACKESPERE tenet per copiam datam xxj die Julij anno xxvij regine Elizabethe unam croftam terre ad edificandum horreum ibidem continentem per estimacionem dimidiam acram terre vocatam Pookecrofte et unum gardinum cum pertinentijs pro termino quinquagenta annorum et reddit per annum . . . . iiij^s viij^d

* * * *

Vicus vocatus Henley strete

JOHANNES SHACKESPERE tenet libere unum tenementum cum pertinentijs per redditum per annum vj^d sectam curie . . . . vj^d

Idem JOHANNES tenet libere unum tenementum per redditum per annum xiij^d sectam curie . . . . ./ . . . . xiij^d

Vicus

Vicus vocatus le Corne strete et Churche strete

WILLIELMUS UNDERHILL GENEROSUS TENET LIBERE QUANDAM DOMUM VOCATAM THE NEWE PLACE CUM PERTINENTIJS PER REDDITUM PER ANNUM xij^d SECTAM CURIE . . . . xij^d

[*Note*—Wm Underhill held also in " Walkers strete unum horreum &^{c}"]

Manerium de Shotterye reddit custumar^9 tenen^9 a Shotterie

JOHANNA HATHEWAY vid tenet per copiam unum messuagium et duas virgatas terre et dimidiam cum pertinentijs per redditum per annum xxxiij iiij^d finem et harriotam . xxxiij^s iiij^d

Manerium de Rowington cum membris customarij tenentes per copiam curie

THOMAS SHACKESPERE tenet per copiam sibi et heredibus suis unum croftum cum pertinentijs per redditum per annum ij^s ad festa predicta equaliter finem, heriotam, sectam curie . . ij^s

Liberi Tenentes

THOMAS SHACKESPERE tenet libere unum mesuagium et unam virgatam terre cum pertinentijs per redditum per annum &c . . . . x^s x^d

Wood end

RICARDUS SHACKSPERE tenet per copiam ut supra

supra unum cottagium et dimidiam virgatam terre et unam acram prati cum pertinentijs per redditum per annum ad festa predicta equaliter vj^s x^d finem et sectam curie . . . . . vj^s x^d

Mulsowe ende

THOMAS SHACKESPERE tenet per copiam ut supra unum mesuagium et unam virgatam terre cum pertinentijs per redditum per annum ad festa predicta equaliter x^s iiij^d finem et harriotam, cum accederit, et sectam curie . . x^s iiij^d

GEORGIUS SHACKESPERE tenet per copiam ut supra unum cottagium et unum croftum terre cum pertinentijs per redditum per annum ad festa predicta equaliter ij^s finem et sectam curie ij^s

RICARDUS SHACKESPERE tenet per copiam ut supra unum mesuagium et dimidiam virgatam terre et duas parcellas prati cum pertinentijs per redditum per annum ad festa predicta equaliter xiiij^s finem et harriotam cum accederit xiiij^s

At the period of the above inquiſition being held, Shakeſpere was twenty-eight years of age. In a ſmall town like Stratford it ſeems that his family had induſtriouſly

"Scattered his Maker's image o'er the land."

There

There was a plentiful supply both of Shakesperes and Hathaways in and about Stratford, not only at that date, but for many years previous. The regifters and records of Rowington and neighbouring parifhes have yielded their evidences to this procreative truth; but the author believes the following quotations from a Mufter Roll of the 28th Henry VIII. (1537), have not previoufly been publifhed:—

Warwyke.

The certyficathe of George Throkmerton knyght John Grevyle Fulke Grevyle Edward Conwey Esquiers and Antony Skynner gent Comyssioners of our souerayne lorde the kings conserninge musters to be taken in the hundred of Barlychwey and libertye of Pathloe in the countye of Warwyke accordinge to the kinges highnes com̃ission to them directed doe certyfie unto your lordships as well the names and surnames of all abell men withine the hundred and libertye aforesaid as horses harnes bowes arows billys and other thinges defensabell and mete for the warre with the diversitie therof whiche ar in every township

of

of the said hundred and libertye that ys to saye

* * * *
ROWINGTON   Able men ther
                         *   *
  (*Inter alios*)   Thomas Shakespere ⎫ Arch[er]
                         *   *   ⎬
                   Ric: Shakespere   ⎭

       *   *   *
WRAXSALL   Able men ther
                         *   *
  (*Inter alios*)   Willm̃ Sakespere   ⎫ Arch[er]
                    *   *   *   ⎬
                   Ric: Shakespere   ⎭

       *   *   *
SHOTERY   Abell men there

                   John Hathewey   ⎫ Arch[er]
                                    ⎭

LOXLEY   Abell men ther

                   Matthew Hathewey ⎫ Arch[er]
                                    ⎭

It will have been obſerved that William Underhill's father (A), the founder of the Idlicote family, was poſſeſſed of an eſtate at Loxley, a hamlet about three miles from Stratford. In this place alſo the

the Hathaways flourifhed, for in the will office at Worcefter the author found the following entries:—

    1541. Hathaway, Thomas . . Loxley.
    1557. Hathway, Simon . . . Loxley.
    1558. Hatheway, Joan . . . Loxley.
    1617. Hathway, John . . . . Loxley.
    1636. Hathway, Richard . . Stratford.
    1637. Hathway, Richard . . Stratford.
    1648. Hathaway, Andrew . . Bellbrougton.

Now, although William Underhill (B), the poffeffor of New Place, had his chief refidence at Idlicote, it feems probable that New Place was a favourite townhoufe with him; and equally probable that it was purchafed as a refidence for him during his father's lifetime, as the fale was effected by his father, three years prior to his death. That death may have occurred much more fuddenly than was ever anticipated; and after his father was laid to reft in Eatington church, William Underhill (B) may have been unwilling

unwilling to retire entirely from a refidence that had only been prepared for his reception three years previoufly. His focial rank and pofition are fufficiently indicated by the preceding inquifition, wherein he is ftyled "generofus;" and the author's reafon for believing that this "William Underhill—generofus" (though actually feated at Idlicote) always kept up his town houfe in Stratford, and occafionally ftayed there, although never making it a fixed refidence, is drawn from the fact, that while the hiftory of the family is to be read in the regifters at Eatington, and the regifters of Stratford are almoft filent, it does fo happen that the author has found one baptifmal entry at Stratford, as follows:—

November 25, 1585.—Elizabeth, daughter of Mr. William Undrell.

The natural inference drawn from this entry being, that during the winter months

months of 1585, the Underhill family removed from Idlicote to their Stratford houfe, at which place it chanced that one of the children was born. We gather from thefe various documents that both at Loxley and in Stratford, William Underhill of New Place was furrounded by Shakefperes and Hathaways. They muft have been familiarly known to him, and he to them; for although there was a broad line of focial demarcation between the yeomen and able-bodied "archers," and the "generofus" mafter of New Place, ftill we muft remember in the cafe of John Shakefpere and his fon there would not be fuch a feparation, becaufe John Shakefpere had attained a pofition in the town fufficiently refpectable to allow of a friendly intimacy exifting between the Underhills and his branch of the Shakefpere family.

From his childhood in 1567 until 1597 Shakefpere

Shakefpere would know William Underhill, Gent., as the owner of New Place.

That he muft have known him focially, and that Underhill muft have had fome private and friendly motive in felling New Place to Shakefpere, almoft upon his death-bed, is a conclufion which the date and circumftances of the fale feem to force upon us. But Shakefpere we know was intimately acquainted with John à Combe, of the " College," and in his will left his fword to Thomas Combe. What of that?

The queftion will be anfwered with the fame explanation which the author would give to the companion queftion, which we can well believe many time-worn lovers of Shakefpere will be inclined to afk: " Why do you burden your book " with a fet of elaborate pedigrees which " no one has given before, and the ufe of " which is not obvious now?"

Let

Let such questions receive this answer. Because the writer believes, honestly and earnestly, that much more fact, and infinitely more probability, concerning Shakespere's life, lies within our reach than is commonly supposed. Heraldry and pedigrees may seem to some persons very dry study; but it may safely be asserted that, despite the flippant jokes of modern democratic writers at the expense of the Herald's Tabard, and the mediæval, quaint associations of the College of Arms, that institution, the Books of Visitations, and the heraldic displays upon ancient church monuments, are becoming daily more and more valuable as contributors to the history of our country. However humorous it may seem to see the *novus homo* of Pie Corner or Pudding Lane assuming a crest to which he has not the remotest pretension, and can show no claim, nevertheless in the

the very affumption there is the indication of an Englifhman's reverence and regard for the ancient landmarks of family and focial hiftory.

What does it matter to any one if the inventor of the lateft Delectable Soap or patentee of the Bifurcating-Baltic-Briftle-Brufh, drops in at one of thofe terrific Holborn fhops, which look like mediæval menageries for the exhibition of crimfon griffins and uproarious gamboge lions; and there, for the fmall charge of 5*s.*, has his "arms found?" What though the brindle cat fits and mews a-top his note-paper, curls its tail upon the flap of his envelopes, and fpreads its whifkers over the handles of his fpoons? Do Garter or Clarenceux lofe their appetites becaufe the vaulting ambition of the fhop has a fneaking love for thefe things, and pays for it in the Queen's taxes, with hair-powder and fuch like?
Not

Not a jot. They know well enough that the honeſt citizen would have found his arms at Doctors' Commons if he could; and that, pleaſe God and his own induſtry, if he can found a family, ſome day or another the brindled cat may have its turn in that direction! Though the cynic may ſmile and ſneer at ſuch cockney pretenſion, and though it has a ludicrous aſpect, nevertheleſs it is not all ludicrous. There is ſomething genuinely Engliſh at the foundation. There is an evidence of the ſpirit of homage to antiquity; of reverence for even the humbleſt aſſociation with anything connected with the records of the country.

As all forms, eccleſiaſtical or civil, have their meaning and their moral, ſo the forms of heraldry—the quainteſt of all—are full of the deepeſt meaning and intereſt. Let the preſent writer make bold to ſay that a moſt intenſely intereſting book might be,

may

may, perhaps, be yet written regarding Shakefpere, by collecting together a record of the perfons and the incidents of thofe perfons' lives with whom the Poet muft of neceffity have been affociated. Thefe pages cannot be devoted to fuch an undertaking; and, therefore, there will be no further attempt made in them than to indicate the direction in which it feems well that fome one fhould travel.

It is by no means impoffible to furround Shakefpere with friends and acquaintances, concerning whom the world generally knows nothing up to the prefent time.

What is the common eftimate of him and of his affociates? Vulgarity is ftamped upon the traditional ftories regarding his life and fociety. We are told he was apprenticed to a butcher. He was a deer-ftealer. He married a woman in a
hurry,

hurry, for a reason about which the less said the better. He lived unhappily with his wife, and as an evidence of his indifference, left her his second-best bed. Last of all, he died of a fever, caught from a bout of drunkenness. Poor Shakespere!

Can any one show that there is a syllable of truth in any of these stories? Do such low-bred vulgarity, immorality, and beastiality, suit with the mind of William Shakespere?

Has he not in his own words supplied for us the vixen-like revenge which littleness, and the worst littleness of all, that of gossips, takes upon any real greatness of mind and character:—" I'll give thee "this plague for thy dowry; be thou as "chaste as ice, as pure as snow, thou "shalt not escape calumny."

Whence do all these stories about our Poet come? Plain, vulgar-tongued folk call

call them—goffip. When ventilated in a fuperior atmofphere, and carried with the beefs and muttons from the fcullery to the dinner-table, the word diffolves into the politer phrafe—tradition. Be it fo! But what is Tradition? Tradition is not to be believed; but always to be confidered. Tradition is a perjured witnefs, who never yet came into court without a lie upon her tongue—for it is a lie to pervert, diftort, exaggerate, or diminifh aught of the truth; and where, either in the memory of man, or on the pages of hiftory, was there ever a piece of "goffip," "town's talk," "what everybody fays," "tradition," that did not, on inveftigation, turn out to be gorged with falfehood?

The ftories current concerning Shake-fpere, which the lapfe of ages has confe-crated with the undeferved title of tradi-tion, might well aftonifh any ftranger to
Englifh

English habits; but they are not in the smallest degree astonishing, when we remember that it is one of the manners and customs of the English to try to knock a man over, the moment he lifts his head above the herd of his fellow-men. If by abuse and slander we can blight his spirit, dull his brain, and break his heart, we give God thanks for having accomplished a worthy, Christian, and charitable end. But if he stands the pelting, and wont be put down, there is a time coming when he can be cuffed and cudgelled to any extent. For your genuine lover of slander—the vampire of private life—the greatest treat on earth is the "post-mortem" of a man's character, whom he has followed with envy, hatred, and malice through life. There are Cannibals, even in England, who want a gospel preaching to them far more than their heathen brethren; for while

while the latter whoop and dance around the dead, and then eat the perifhing flefh, the former exultingly leap upon, and until they are fick with furfeit, devour the more than body—the reputation, the life in death, of thofe who lie defencelefs in the grave.

There is no need to be furprifed that even mighty Shakefpere's memory has been handed down to us blackened and defamed by goffip. In inverfe ratio, the higher a man attains, the lower and bafer he is likely to be reprefented. An unerring gauge whereby to meafure the value of character and genius againft goffip, in the cafe of Shakefpere, is here fupplied.

The ftory—which will hereafter be referred to—regarding the caufes which led to Shakefpere's death, is generally familiar, and has, as a matter of courfe, been commonly reported in Stratford. In order to
fhow

show how gossip—otherwise tradition—improves as she passes from mouth to mouth, the author lately encountered the statement, gravely made to him by a clergyman at Luddington, who had been assured of its truth, that "Shake-"spere died drunk." That assertion will read to every one as wicked and preposterous as it sounded in the ears of the writer. But why wicked and preposterous? It is the natural result, and inevitable development of the story told in the Rev. Mr. Ward's Diary, which need not be further discussed in this place. This piece of gossip of 1862, the author believes precisely to the same extent that he does any and all of the before-mentioned stories. They all rest upon one basis, and that basis is a rotten one.

A very clever, and, in its way, a very convincing pamphlet, was published a short

Stratford-upon-Avon. 115

short time back, by Charles Holte Bracebridge, Esq., entitled "Shakespeare no "Deerstealer," the gift of which is, that Shakespere did not kill the deer in Charlecote at all, but in Fulbroke Park; that in so doing he committed no offence against the law, or morals, but that he offended Sir Thomas Lucy thereby. Mr. Bracebridge quotes the statement of the late Mr. Lucy to Sir Walter Scott, that "the park from which Shakespere stole "the buck was not that which surrounds "Charlecote."

Mr. Bracebridge's pamphlet is well worth reading, and he has done good service by it to the memory of the Poet.

Now as to the value of tradition. Though tradition invariably speaks falsely, as in one instance Mr. Bracebridge has shown, nevertheless, though a wretched bad witness in court to give evidence, she serves as a very useful sign-post upon the

the highways of time. She commonly (not always) points to something that deserves inquiring into, and indicates the direction in which we shall find it worth our while to travel. So with regard to the traditions about Shakespere: the author believes they are a mixture of absurdity and of falsehood; but at the same time, while rejecting them as at all trustworthy, they seem to him to serve a useful purpose in exciting inquiry, and making us seek for the truth that underlies them. As evil is commonly good perverted, so falsehood is often the wicked or idle misrepresentation of something true at bottom; and as good as it is true.

Let any one of the so-called traditions concerning Shakespere be brought into court, and searchingly examined, and it will be committed for perjury.

But let us take the rambling old tercentenarian

centenarian crone at her real value; go and fit with her in her timber and plaster cottage at Stratford, and liften to her as fhe told her ftory to Betterton, or to Ward, or in her later years to Malone or Stevens, and we fhall thank her, not for what fhe teaches us, but for fending us off in the right direction in purfuit of fomething we have yet to learn.

There is Mr. John Shakefpere, in Henley Street—he is a glover, or a butcher, or a "yeoman," or wool-dealer!—what is he? Can no one fum up all the fuppofed trades or bufineffes, and fay in a word, that they moft probably mean he was a woolftapler? Make him of any one of the above trades actually and folely, and we cannot reconcile the other ftatements.

But like the variorum readings of the fame names and the fame employments in Shakefpere's days, if we
adopt

adopt the conclusion that he was a Merchant of the Staple, we shall easily be able to understand his being called both butcher and glover. Considering what a staple trade gloving was in John Shakespere's time, in his own county, if he were connected with the mercers in London, he would of necessity deal in gloves. The possessor of land, and the owner of cattle, it is the height of probability that he may have slaughtered his sheep in his own farm-yard, in order to have the skins properly preserved. Butcher he might easily be called, and so might his son William; and also be represented as apprenticed to a butcher, when he was in reality apprenticed to his father.

So, again, the story about Shakespere killing an animal, or helping to kill one, may be true in origin, but tradition's representation of it be as untrue, as if one of our princes or peers were nominated

nated a "butcher" becaufe he happened to be prefent when a ftag's throat was cut.

And fo, again, there is the deer ftory. Mr. Bracebridge may be right as far as he goes; and yet, while tradition points to fome fact that did occur, he might perhaps, though wanting evidence, and yet in truth, have gone much further. Might not Shakefpere have been out, not merely for fport, but as a matter of bufinefs? Might not his father have regularly killed, and paid for deer out of Fulbroke Park? Might not the quarrel with Sir Thomas Lucy have arifen upon this ground; and an imperious, hot-headed country fquire have attempted to interfere with Shakefpere, thereby making himfelf ridiculous, and henceforward becoming famous in his folly?

Again, as regards Shakefpere's removal to London. May not that have happened

pened for bufinefs motives? and may he not, during his whole London career, have benefited by a profitable trade, that gave him the pofition of a gentleman, and connected him with gentlemen? and alfo enabled him to realife that independence upon which he retired? It muft never be forgotten that his father was in difficulties about the time when the Poet removed to the metropolis; and from that moment we never again hear of, or trace any domeftic anxieties in the houfe of John Shakefpere. The inference feems conclufive.

Look at Shakefpere, in his home-life at Stratford: is he not continually engaged in commercial tranfactions—buying and felling corn, buying land, farms, tythes? Shakefpere was a bufy man—an active, thrifty, accumulative man. He was evidently anxious to make money, and to found a family. His will, and the
records

records of Heralds' College, in his father's grant of arms, prove this.

When he became more permanently refident at Stratford, we find him exhibiting the habits of life previoufly contracted. Men's habits are not changed in mid-life, and new ones affumed. What Shakefpere was at Stratford we have every reafon to fuppofe he was in London; but whatever the fources of his accumulations, whether from one or various fources—the ftage, his plays, and commercial enterprifes—we *know* that he did make money; and that at a very early time of life he was able to eftablifh himfelf and family in New Place. So far from the vulgar, bafelefs conjecture, that Shakefpere ran off to London to avoid Sir Thomas Lucy having anything to recommend it, it feems to the author as far-fetched and prepofterous, as it is totally devoid of a fcintilla of evidence in its favour.

Why

Why should we delight in perpetuating such miserable fudge? Why should one writer after another, and one generation after another, pass on, from book to book, and from mouth to mouth, a set of stories that would be (divested of the grand-sounding epithet "tradition," and branded with their proper designation, —pot-house gossip) rejected as only suited to the ideas of tap-room topers? The term is used advisedly. There is the faint, oppressive odour of that region— saturated with the stench of stale beer, and the despoiling of men's reputations— about almost all the "traditions" of Shakespere. Shakespere with merry companions, over the "cheerful bowl," is perpetually being presented to our notice by tradition. Shakespere, and "the science of drinking (at Bidford) the largest quantity of liquor without being intoxicated!" Shakespere dead-drunk, and sleeping the
night

night through "under the umbrageous "boughs of a crab-tree!" Shakefpere making doggrel verfes at the expenfe of his particular and perfonal friend, at a tavern, faid to have been known by the fign of "the Bear!" Shakefpere drinking too hard at a merry-meeting, and dying thereby of a fever!

Oh! pundits of our literature! biographers of the greateft man of all your craft! lovers of the Saxon tongue! is it by fuch boozing tales as thefe that ye honour the High Prieft of your profeffion? Muft the incenfe that you offer at his fhrine reek with the coarfe odour of the village politician's and wifeacre's foul tobacco, and ftill fouler breath? Can no Neibuhr of Englifh record be found ftrong enough and manly enough to cleanfe the ftream of hiftory, by purifying and contemptuous ridicule of this corrupting garbage, polluting everything

thing with its poisonous "tradition?" We are taught to distrust an autograph of Shakespere's, and cautioned not to believe a scrap of writing to be true, unless there is internal corroborative evidence to establish its authority! Better, surely, to caution the world against believing a scrap of vulgar gossip, unless there is some internal, and corroborative evidence to establish its authenticity. No one is a jot the worse or better whether a line of writing be genuine or forged; but a whole nation is made worse,—every man who speaks the Saxon tongue is worse, because his confidence and respect are shaken, if he discover that the teacher of the highest, noblest thoughts—the Poet who fills the heart with admiration for all that is noble and virtuous and honourable in human nature, began life as a thief, spent it as a vagabond, and ended it as a drunkard! Softer-spoken words might be culled from the

the dictionary; but these are the real and simple terms by which, in plain, unvarnished speech, Shakespere deserves to be described, if the self-condemning "traditions" in common currency regarding him are to be reproduced and re-believed.

It may be said, that the author has met tradition by nothing better than suggestion and that any one can draw pictures from imagination. But this would hardly be just. Which sort of evidence is more agreeable and acceptable,—that which is probably true because it rests upon conclusions derived from known facts; or that which is probably untrue, because it rests upon no other foundation than the loose and shifting stories of gossips?

Gossip represents Shakespere as a boozing and beer-drinking fellow. Facts do not prove that he was not; but facts provide us with evidences of his energy, labour,

labour, and thrift, leading us to conclusions from those facts which convince us he could not possibly have been so. *Ex uno disce omnes!* Gossip says he was a deer-stealer in Charlecote Park: facts now prove that statement to be positively false, and that if he killed a deer at Fulbroke, Sir Thomas Lucy had no power to prevent him. Gossip says he ran away to avoid the knight's displeasure; facts prove that his father was a man in considerable repute, connected with the Mercer's trade, but that he got into difficulties; and at that precise period we find young Shakespere went to London. Facts truly do not prove, but they lead us to a reasonable conclusion based upon them, that Shakespere went to London for good and honest purposes; and that he went as a man of business, not as a homeless vagrant is the more probable, because facts show that his father retained possession

sion of his residence, and we hear no more of his troubles; while in a brief period of time his son returned to Stratford, able to establish himself in the "Great House" there.

Let us judge of Shakspere by what we really know of him, however small and circumscribed the amount of our information may be. Rejecting with scorn the old wives' fables, which other old wives seem to have delighted in perpetuating, it is a safer and more honourable path to pursue, if we set out upon a journey in search of facts, and, like Pilgrim, ease our shoulders of that bundle of fictions which have burdened us. Let tradition be a finger-post, and nothing more! If the enthusiastic lovers of the Poet would content themselves with healthy exercise, they might perhaps find that there are still many facts waiting to be dug out of ancient records that have been brushed
past

past by us ten thousand times, and yet never detected. The silver mines of Potosi were discovered by the tearing aside of a bramble; and yet their treasures had laid through the long centuries close to the handling of men. So it may prove that there are treasures of history that have been very close to some among us, which an accident some day may disclose. Even though it be not so, the subject is well worth diligent search.

It seems extraordinary that many of the rapturous admirers of the genius of the Poet perpetuate, as if they were true, so many vulgar slanders and gossips regarding the man. If they were true, we might begin to suspect there is something after all in that strange theory that Shakespere's plays were never written by Shakespere, but by Francis Bacon; because it would be impossible to reconcile the man that we should picture from the

writings

writings, with the man that we should know in his acts. In Mr. Charles Knight's most interesting "Biography of "Shakespere" and running commentary upon contemporary history, manners, and habits of the country, a proper and contemptuous protest is entered against the ungracious doggrel attributed to Shakespere, as written at the expense of his friend and neighbour John à Combe, an estimable, worthy, and charitable gentleman, whom tradition has nicknamed usurer! Usurer! Let any one read his Will, and it will be seen what a friend the poor of Stratford had in the kind old man who lived among them, and bountifully bequeathed his property for their benefit. The good that he did, has, indeed, been interred with his bones.

This story, and others, Mr. Knight has dismissed as they deserve. It is heartily to be desired that many more of the
Poet's

Poet's biographers had done, and would ſtill do, the ſame.

Can no other picture of him be drawn? Let us make the attempt.

It will be admitted that Shakeſpere was a precocious and ambitious youth. Let the motive for his early marriage have been what it may, there was precocity in the ſtep. But if we diſcard the diſhonouring ſuggeſtions that have been made regarding it, and conſider it as the act of a young man who had a ſolemn and earneſt appreciation of the value and purpoſe of life, we ſhall find that ſuch a view of the tranſaction harmoniſes with the whole of Shakeſpere's conduct. Let it be ſaid—it matters not—that this is taking a very novel view of his conduct: is it not better, when we are attributing motives to a perſon, to try and find good rather than bad ones? Shakeſpere, it is true, needs no apologiſt, leaſt of all the advocacy

vocacy of so feeble a pen as that which traces these lines; but to furnish motives for a man's acts is a pastime at which all can play an even game; and therefore the fancy of one man is just as good as that of another. The Poet's character is read from a totally different point of view in these pages to that taken by De Quincey and by many others.* Let it be pardoned, if in love and admiration the author seems presumptuous when he says, that he considers, in the glorification of the poet, Shakespere's character has wanted staunch and faithful champions,—men

"To think no slander; no, nor listen to it."

Let the suggestion above made be entertained for a moment, and in what a totally different light do the two momentous actions of the Poet's life present themselves! —his early marriage, and his early setting out

---

* Appendix I.

out for London to fight circumſtance and conquer independence!

Precocity and ambition are herein combined. Who shall blame them? This man commenced life as a good man ſhould begin it: there was no "ſowing of wild oats;" no libertiniſm; no exhauſtion of the ſtrength of youth amidſt the ſtews of a metropolis. Let Shakeſpere's acts—the facts of his life—be weighed againſt the words of goſſips who never knew him, and the author contends thoſe facts all go to turn the ſcale in his favour.

His firſt ſtep on the threſhold of manhood argues the ſenſe of reſponſibility, and the ambition for reſpectability. It was in the man; and it came out and ſhowed itſelf at the earlieſt poſſible moment.*

There

---

* When it was ſtated, at p. 31, that there are two ſeals to Shakeſpere's marriage bond, one bearing the impreſſion "R.H.," it would have been more correct to ſay there "were," becauſe the ſeals have entirely vaniſhed, and there is ſcarcely a trace of them on the parchment.

Stratford-upon-Avon. 133

There is another charaćteriſtic—the granting of arms to Shakeſpere's father. It

---

parchment. Nearly fourteen years have elapſed ſince the author laſt heard anything of that bond, and it was only by accident that, being in Worceſter lately, he took the opportunity to give it a freſh examination. On doing ſo, he compared the text of Mr. Halliwell and Mr. Knight with the original, and found that the copy (given at pp. 29, 30) is perfećtly correćt, while that of Mr. Knight ("Biography," p. 275) contains theſe errors :—

"By reaſon of any p̄contraćt or affinitie, or by any other," &c., inſtead of "by reaſon of any p̄contraćt, conſanquitie, affinitie," &c.

"May lawfully ſolemnize m̄riony," inſtead of "may lawfully ſolemnize m̄riony together."

"Laws in that caſe provided," inſtead of "lawes in that behalf provided."

With regard to Luddington, as the probable place of Shakeſpere's marriage, it may be well to put it on record that there is ſtill living an old gentleman, named Pidering, at Colton, near Alceſter, who, when a youth, reſided at Luddington. This perſon diſtinćtly remembers having heard it poſitively aſſerted by the inhabitants of the hamlet that Shakeſpere was married in their chapel; and he alſo remembers the books and regiſters of the chapel being burnt in a fire which occurred at his couſin's, the chapelwarden's houſe, *at the commencement of the preſent century.* (*Query.* Did Malone ever ſearch thoſe books?) Mr. Baldwin, who now occupies the farm on Luddington Green, preſerves the remains of a Gothic font which belonged to the chapel, as alſo the Black-letter Bible which belonged to the reading-deſk, and the key of the porch, which was dug up a few years ſince in the garden which now covers the ruins.

It is univerfally admitted that this was Shakefpere's act; and that it was he who prompted John Shakefpere's application to Herald's College.

It will be obferved upon the Shakefpere Pedigree, that the condition of his anceftors and the grants of lands, as recorded in the draft of the pedigree in Herald's College, have been reproduced as correct, attributing them to the favour of Henry VII., to whom John Shakefpere's great-grandfather did faithful and approved fervice. William Dethick, Garter Principal King-at-Arms, has been charged with granting arms improperly; and Mr. Halliwell particularly dwells upon the fcoring and interlining of the original grant of 1596. It feems to the author that this fcoring and correction was moft natural, and that in all probability it occurred from the fact of the evidence being taken down from the lips of William Shakefpere. Dethick

Dethick is not to be charged with the falsehood or misrepresentation, if any, appearing in the two drafts of arms, dated 1596 and 1599. In both these the faithful services of the Shakesperes to King Henry VII. is solemnly asserted; and it is hard to believe that the assertion is untrue, when it agrees so well with the probable settlement of the Shakesperes in Warwickshire, and was made, almost beyond doubt, by the Poet personally, to Dethick, since the draft bears date when Shakespere was busy in London, and the *year before he purchased New Place*—a significant fact!

Therefore, on the Pedigree in this book, that statement is accepted and believed, because the author believes the draft was drawn under information provided by William Shakespere himself; and he believes likewise that the man, with the chivalric feelings of a gentleman, would have scorned to tell a lie.

It

It has been suggested that because, as it will be seen, the Ardens served King Henry VII., Shakespere was confounding his maternal with his paternal ancestors. So that we may take our choice as to whether, in the first case, he was a liar; or, in the second, a fool. Pleasing alternatives for those who relish them! But it is to be hoped there are not wanting believers in the candour and truthfulness of the Poet; who, like Mr. C. Knight, in his "Biography," accept with credit the statement found in both the drafts, for which we must hold Shakespere himself responsible, confidently believing that it was supplied as information by him in the drawing of the first draft of 1596, and repeated by Garter King in 1599.

But what was the motive for Shakespere instigating his father to obtain this grant? It can hardly fail to be obvious

to

to any mind that is not tortuous. The author believes that the grant was fought with the same motive that the early marriage was contracted,—that New Place was purchased,—and that Shakespere's will, finally, was made. It seems to him that in all these things, and in his wonderful mental activity and positive labour, there was the one noble, worthy, ambitious motive throughout: Shakespere wished to found a family. He loved from his early days the honoured respectability of an English gentleman. He long ed and desired that his family should achieve a place among the gentry of Warwickshire. The ambition that we have seen in the present century, at Abbotsford, was precisely what was seen at New Place in 1597. Perhaps there is a more extended parallel between Scott and Shakespere than this. Was there not the same historic feeling in both these men?
The

The love for antiquity, for defcent, for heraldry, for chivalric ftory and incident, is confpicuous in each of them! Shakefpere's plays are hiftoric chronicles; fo are Scott's novels. They prefent in a popular form, to the entrancement of the people, a moving fpectacle of events of which many would otherwife be profoundly ignorant. It requires a peculiar fympathy of mind to deal with fuch fubjects,—and that *thorough fympathy* was inbred in the characters of Shakefpere and Scott.

No carelefs reader of Shakefpere's works can poffibly mifs obferving the antiquary's tafte that pervades them. Let this be carried in memory, and the pride of anceftry, in the draft of the grant of arms, will be recognifed as his natural characteriftic, and not as Dethick's invention.

It will be obferved that the author treats with abfolute difbelief and difguft

guft the "traditions" current concerning the Poet; and he is impatient of them, becaufe he folemnly believes them to be injurious to the credit which the Man, as diftinct from the Poet, deferves to enjoy among his countrymen. He believes that the known and authenticated facts of Shakefpere's life, taken by themfelves, prefent to us a Character to be refpected and loved, juft as much as his works do a Poet to be admired. Of thofe leading events of Shakefpere's life which have been fummarifed above, he conceives that, when any mind difengages itfelf from the mire of tradition, they can only be regarded in one light,—to his honour and fair fame.

This is a mighty contraft and contradiction to the currently-received ftories about ftealing deer, marrying in fhame, and running away to London! But thofe are ftories without confirmation or evidence,

dence, and the author holds they are pofitively irreconcilable with the proved and authentic facts of Shakefpere's life, which uniformly exhibit him as an induftrious, high-minded, afpiring citizen, and a man ambitious of taking rank with the families of Englifh gentry.

We are informed by Rowe, who gives the ftory on the authority of Sir William Davenant, that Lord Southampton, out of his great friendfhip for Shakefpere, prefented him with £1000, to enable him to make a purchafe for which he had a mind. This gift is fuppofed to have been made fome time fubfequent to the year 1593, when "Venus and Adonis" was publifhed, and dedicated to his lordfhip!

We float aloft into a higher and purer atmofphere when we picture our Shakefpere winning and holding fuch an "efpecial friend,"—being focially connected with fuch a man as Southampton; and befriended

befriended by William and Philip Herbert, Earls of Pembroke and Montgomery.

Something too much has been written about the inferior pofition of the Poet; and that pofition has been kept down by the everlafting low-lived ftories with which his name has been begrimed.

Shakefpere's genius needs no eulogies. It were to paint the lily to laud that. But *Shakefpere*—the man, the citizen, the high-minded polifhed gentleman, ambitious of pofition and afferting his title to affociate with gentlemen—this is a perfon of whom we have heard too little. From all that his biographers have commonly put before us, we might naturally conclude that he was a fort of dramatic penny-a-liner, fcribbling by day from neceffity—at the point of the literary bayonet—the pen—a certain amount of "copy," the value of which was unknown to himfelf, and delighting at night in the fottifh fociety of taverns.

taverns. It may be that on thefe pages this picture of him is expofed in a broader and more glaring light than the public are accuftomed to fee it in. The author afferts that it is the true light; and believes that the focial and moral portraiture of the man, as painted by "tradition" (fifh-wives' goffip), is as grofs and prepofterous as he alfo believes every one of thofe daubs, (Chandos or otherwife), which are foifted on the public as likeneffes of the phyfical man, are like fign-painters' portraits, having far lefs relation to the original than the "Saracen's Head" had to Sir Roger de Coverley. Is there not more fatisfaction in contemplating Shakefpere as the efpecial friend of Southampton, than as regarding him as the "hale-fellow, well-met" companion of the fwilling chaw-bacons of "Piping Pebworth, Dancing Marfton," &c. &c.?

Talk of reverence for this mighty man's

man's works!—it seems there is plenty of lack of reverence for the man himself.

Let us ask ourselves, when we prate about our love for the "Immortal Bard," where we find anything to justify our base-born traditional rubbish about that Immortal Man? Shakespere could not have acquired the independence he did, had he not been a sober, cleanly-living, thrifty man.

Shakespere could not have instigated his father to acquire that coat-of-arms, had he not been an ambitious man: ambitious in the purest and best sense of that word —ambitious to raise himself in social position and respect.

Shakespere would not have completed the purchase of such a property as New Place, and have made it his permanent residence, unless he had been what we now call commercially "a thoroughly respectable man," anxious to take his
place

place amongst gentlemen, and to be esteemed as "generosus" in his own county.

Every *known fact* of his life goes to support these assertions. Let fact be weighed in the scale with fable, and the measure of the man will give us for result a character to respect, as well as a genius to admire.

Something has been said in allusion to Heraldry. There is one source of indirect information regarding Shakespere which has never as yet been thoroughly examined. Authors and biographers have riddled through the sieve of criticism every grain of direct evidence regarding him, known of, and available. Close Rolls, Records, Inquisitions, Registers, have surrendered their silent testimonies. But Fines, Leases, Sales, Births, Deaths, and Marriages, while they give us direct and positive knowledge, do not give that indirect testimony

Stratford-upon-Avon. 145

mony to be gathered from contemporary affociation. A Pedigree, quaint and formal as it may look, when well read and ftudied, may yet be found to guide the antiquary's fearch in fome direction rich with indirect, and leading perchance to the moft direct, evidence regarding the Poet.

As thefe lines are being penned, there lie before the writer twelve hundred clofely-written foolfcap fheets of Warwickfhire pedigrees and family hiftories, compiled by the late Rev. Thomas Warde, Vicar of Wefton-under-Wetherley and of Barford, Warwickfhire. They are a part of the labour of a long life of an enthufiaftic antiquary's refearch. They are interfperfed with pen-and-ink fketches of ancient Warwickfhire timber-houfes, many of which are now deftroyed; and their pages are crowded with the moft interefting family and local records, fuch as have not

not been collected together by any one since Sir W. Dugdale published his famous book, despite its numerous errors. When the author first perused this MS., his intention was to quote from it largely; but he has relinquished that idea, partly because to do so properly would have involved the publication of a work of magnitude; and partly because in doing so it would have been robbing the MS. itself of riches, which, in the author's opinion, would have been like rifling the tomb of the dead of its treasure. Whole and undefiled the Rev. Mr. Warde's MS. shall remain, until such time as its precious and singularly interesting pages can be given entire to the public; though that portion of the public which takes interest in such matters will grieve to hear that the documents now confided to the author's charge do not form more than a quarter of the number which once existed, and

perished

Stratford-upon-Avon.

perished in a fire in London some years ago. From the pages of the fragment of twelve hundred sheets still preserved, many items of information contained in this volume have been gathered; and a store of detail regarding the Lucys, Underhills, Combes, Boughtons, Shirleys, Cloptons, Carews, Grevilles, Throckmortons, and others who lived in Shakespere's time, has proved to the author the value of the opinion he now expresses, as to the wide field of indirect evidence still to be explored, calculated to convey most interesting information, that may lead to a far more perfect knowledge of Shakespere himself than the present age possesses.

The names just given (and many others of the Warwickshire gentry might be added), when we study them by the help of the College of Arms, are found linked together by intermarriages, bringing before us curious and interesting facts elsewhere

where unattainable; and repeopling the paft by fuch aid, we are enabled to furround Shakefpere with the forms and figures of men and women who, in the nature of things, muft have known him well, and been known by him. The names of Sir Thomas Lucy, William Combe, Sir Thomas Throckmorton, and Fulke Greville pafs before us as Members for the county of Warwick. By turning to the Clopton Pedigree, we find John Combe married to Rofe Clopton, of Clopton.* On the tomb of Judith Combe, in Stratford, we find the arms of Combe quartered with Underhill, and the hiftory of the two families puts before us the intermarriages. In the fame way we learn of the alliance between the daughter of Sir Stephen Hales, the contemporary of Shakefpere, and Edward Combe.
Again,

---

* Appendix J.

Again, the grandson of Thomas Underhill married the daughter of Sir William Lucy. And again, Jocosa, or Joyce Clopton (three years younger than Shakespere, born 1568), married George Carew, afterwards Earl of Totnes. These were people associated with Stratford, with many of whom Shakespere must have been familiar. The Combes, the Underhills, the Cloptons, the Carews, it may be asserted without any hesitation, were his friends. What does the world know of these people? It has heard John Combe libelled as a usurer; and been told that he was Shakespere's friend until the Poet lampooned him. It has learned that the Earl of Totnes was a brave soldier. And this is all. The evidence of John Combe's regard for Shakespere has paled before a doggrel verse. The evidence of Shakespere's attachment to the Combes has been made nothing of.
The

New Place,

The fact that Lord Totnefs, living at Clopton Houfe, was a man of letters and an author, has efcaped notice beyond the record of the fact itfelf. And the ftory that Lord Southampton prefented Shakefpere with £1000 to complete a purchafe on which he had fet his heart, has never, it is believed, been pointed at the acquirement of New Place.

When people have been fufficiently naufeated with the fentimental rubbifh with which the prefs has teemed about the "Immortal Bard," and when the tap-room talk, yclept tradition, has been poured out into the gutter with its kindred dregs, the healthy and honeft refearches of the good and true fearchers of this age after fact, will lead to the gathering of new materials for writing the hiftory of Shakefpere. In fo doing it will be well to furround him with the focial facts of Stratford at the time when he lived, having

Stratford-upon-Avon. 151

having ſtripped him of the fables of half a century after he died. It is ſurely more profitable to know the perſons among whom he dwelt, than to liſten to the looſe ſtatements of people that he never ſaw. Inquiries about his contemporaries may bring us to diſcover ſomething about *him;* but if they never teach us anything poſitive as to his hiſtory, there is ſome ſatisfaction in contemplating the men and women who had the privilege of his acquaintance.

Let us glance at one or two of the Stratford worthies of the Shakeſperian age.

There were three houſes which we of the preſent generation would give much to have reſcued from deſtruction: New Place, the Poet's home; the College of Stratford, the home of his friend John à Combe; Clopton Houſe, the home of the Cloptons and Carews. Of theſe three, two have utterly periſhed: the third,
Clopton

Clopton Houfe, exifts as it was reconftructed by Sir Edward Walker (F) in the time of Charles II. Happily one morfel of the original houfe, built in the time of Henry VII., has been fpared. It ftands at the back of the prefent manfion, and was a porch-way entrance acrofs the ancient moat. One hundred and forty years have paffed away fince a Sir Hugh Clopton (H), and withal a Herald of the College of Arms, deftroyed the houfe in which Shakefpere died. The prefent generation, therefore, has been robbed of nothing which it has contemplated and poffeffed. Not fo with the College. That venerable ftructure, erected in the reign of Edward III. by Ralph de Stratford, Bifhop of London, and adjoining the yard of Stratford Church, was fhamefully deftroyed within the memory of living men. This monaftic eftablifhment had been "embellifhed" at the
front

front towards the church, with Georgian facing; but at the back it ftill retained many of its mediæval architectural features. Unfortunately, in the year 1796, it was fold to one Edmund Batterfbee, a man who had made money in Manchefter, and curfed Stratford by fettling there. The MS. records in the author's truft, allude to the College as follows :—

"In 1797, the furniture of this
" manfion, the College, was difpofed of
" by auction, together with a collection
" of paintings. Many of them were very
" curious, ancient, and valuable; and
" fome very interefting family portraits,
" which were, unfortunately for the
" antiquary, fold and difperfed. Whole
" lengths of Queen Elizabeth, Charles II.
" and his Queen, Louis XIII. and his
" Queen. Charles II. and his Queen,
" Louis and his, are now in the Town
                                  " Hall

"Hall at Lichfield, having been purchased
"for a trifle each, for Mr. Green's
"museum in that town, and since its
"being discontinued, these pictures—*not
"finding a purchaser!*—have been all
"hung up in the Town Hall. Full
"length paintings of George, Prince of
"Denmark, George I., and II. also de-
"corated this antique mansion. A large
"piece, bearing the date 1641. A half-
"length portrait of Juxon, Bishop of
"London, who attended the unfortunate
"King Charles I. to the scaffold. This
"painting very likely was an original, as
"the pious Bishop, at the time of the
"usurpation of Cromwell, retired to his
"house at Little Compton, in Gloucef-
"tershire, which is not far from Strat-
"ford. A very beautiful half-length
"portrait of Lady Radnor, *and innume-
"rable family portraits!* and others too
"numerous to mention.

"This

"This venerable manfion,—which had
" exifted through a lapfe of 446 years,
" and fince the fuppreffion of the religious
" houfes in the reign of Henry VIII.
" had been the refidence of feveral very
" honourable families,—was now doomed
" to fall, and its ancient walls to be
" pulled down to the ground, though the
" whole of the manfion was in perfect
" repair, and fome parts of it fitted up in
" the modern ftyle by its purchafer, who
" very unfortunately had purchafed it.
" Being an entire ftranger to the town of
" Stratford, having lately purchafed the
" houfe ftanding near the large gates of
" the entrance to the church, where he
" refided, and having more money than
" any regard for venerable antiquity, or
" any refpect for antiquarian lore, or the
" ancient poffeffors of this noble manfion,
" he, tradefman-like,—for he was a Man-
" chefter tradefman,—not liking that the
"ground

"ground facing his own houfe fhould be encumbered with fuch an old antiquated building, determined to have the whole pulled down, like Mr. Gaftrell, who deftroyed the famous mulberry-tree. By the taking down of this ancient pile the town of Stratford had to lament the deprivation of one of the chief and greateft ornaments. But Mr. Batterfbee, regardlefs of public opinion, and defirous of the land on which it ftood, to make ufe of part for a kitchen-garden and the reft for pafture for his cattle, deftroyed the whole of the old College in 1800. *Sic tranfit, &c.*"

The above quotation has been made in full, that the reader may have a fpecimen of the ruthlefs manner in which, little more than half a century ago, the moft interefting family reliques were difperfed, and the houfe in which Shakefpere had fpent many an hour with the Combes and the

the Cloptons was deſtroyed! Can it be that when old ſwords, and halberds, and ruſting antiquities were turned out with the pots and kettles, Shakeſpere's ſword went along with them? *It is quite poſſible.*

Paſs we on now to Clopton Houſe, which, happily, remains. As before ſtated, one remnant of the antique Shakeſperian edifice ſtill ſtands: the remainder of the manſion being Carolean. Neſtling under the weſtern ſweep of Welcombe Hills, the ſlopes rich with verdure, dotted with copſes, and ſhadowed with ancient trees, among which the deer feed, ſtands Clopton Houſe. As we look upon that ſolitary remnant of the Tudor Houſe, we feel a thrill of pleaſure in the conviction that under its portal Shakeſpere and his friends muſt have paſſed ſcores of times. The moat ran directly in front of it, and was a few years back diſturbed, in
order

order to lay fome modern foundations. Various trifling reliques of by-gone days were recovered, and among others three fack-bottles of ftunted form, made of the coarfeft glafs. Two of them had the creft of Combe upon them. There is a theme for a reverie! Sack from the College, taken up to the Houfe! Was it an offering from John à Combe to Lord Totnefs? Was it a fpecial prefent at fome Chriftmas time, when the lips of the Lady Joyce or the Poet pledged the cup, and did honour to the "Boar's "Head?" Who can tell? The empty bottles funk in the mud of a moat for centuries come back to light, and tell us on what friendly terms the families of Combe and Clopton were, in the days when they pledged the toaft in fack.*

There

---

* One of thefe bottles is now in poffeffion of the author. From the length of time that it has been buried, it has acquired thofe prifmatic colours which grow upon glafs under the foil.

There is but one place left which, in its reliques and affociations, brings Shakefpere vividly back to the imagination, and that is Clopton Houfe!

We enter its noble hall, with receffed bay-window full of the Clopton coats of arms, and running our eyes round the walls we light upon the manly, maffive head of George Carew, Lord Totnefs. There hangs his portrait as frefh, and in as fine prefervation as the day it was painted.* There, too, are numerous members of the Clopton family—Joyce, the Countefs, venerable men, and noble ladies, coming down in fucceffion to Mr. and Mrs. Partheriche. There is a fplendid original of the "Lady Elizabeth," Cromwell's

---

* There are two portraits of Lord Carew at Clopton Houfe. The one here referred to came from Afton Hall, Birmingham; the other, which has always been in the houfe, hangs in one of the galleries. Both pictures feem to have been painted at one date, and the treatment is the fame; but the Afton is in far the beft prefervation.

Cromwell's mother: and a moſt intereſting painting of the river front of Whitehall Palace in the days of the Stuarts. Among a multitude of others, is a beautiful portrait of Sir Edward Walker, wearing his badge of Garter King.

In turning over the papers and MSS. of Clopton Houſe the author met with an ancient written and *emendated* copy of the third part of " Jewel's Apology!"

What ſtory could this manuſcript tell! It is in the handwriting of the time of Mary and Elizabeth. Whoſe was the book? Could it ever have belonged to Jewel himſelf, or was it made for ſome member of this Clopton family? Who can gueſs?

Perhaps the moſt precious book of all at Clopton is a ſmall volume by Richard Pynſon—a collection of Statutes. It is as complete and perfect as the day it iſſued from the preſs of the King's Printer. This

This book tranfports us back to Shakefpere's own times. It was in his day exactly what we fee it now. Whence it came, whofe it was, none can tell. But it is among the old books and papers of fuch a place as Clopton that we beft like to meet with fuch a book. Tumbling about in unknown nooks and corners there may yet be found other fuch, and more direct evidences connected both with the Poet's period and the Poet himfelf. Here, at leaft, is one book publifhed before Shakefpere's birth, which we find preferved not only in Warwickfhire, but in the very houfe with which all his circle of friends is affociated. Let the fact fpeak for itfelf.

From the houfes let us glance at their mafters and miftreffes!

Much ftrefs has been laid upon heraldic refearch, and the author,—it may be fomewhat boldly, but, neverthelefs, very fincerely,—

cerely,—has expreffed not merely his opinion about the value of heraldic records, upon which there needs no opinion to be expreffed; but his conviction that there is yet much knowledge to be gained from refearches, to which a comparifon of the Warwickfhire pedigrees of Shakefpere's age, would lead the inquirer. In preparing thefe pages for the Prefs, the examination of the Vifitations has led the author again and again upon the track of information of which he was previoufly in utter ignorance. May not the fame refult await other inquirers? Moreover, we experience a frefhened intereft when we gain a knowledge of the perfons who furround the Poet in familiar intercourfe. That marriage regifter—

"1561. June 4.—Johannes Combes, *Generosus*, "et Rosa Cloptonne"—

brings Shakefpere into connection with the great folk at Clopton from his earlieft years.

Stratford-upon-Avon. 163

years. Rofe was married the year after her father died, and her brother William had come into poffeffion. She was miftrefs of the College during the firft fifteen years of the Poet's life, and as fhe watched him growing, and faw him attain his fourth year, fhe would hear the news from the Houfe that her brother's wife had brought him a little girl—duly chriftened Jocofa or Joyce. This was the future Countefs. The Poet would be juft old enough to remember her being born, the year after William Underhill, Efquire, had come to refide at New Place. The boy and girl grew up to man's and woman's eftate, familiar with the fame people and having the fame friends. In 1575, Queen Elizabeth arrived at Kenilworth, and Mafter Langham, in his letter to Mafter Martin defcribing the Queen's vifit, difcovered that "Olld Hags, prying into every place, "are az fond of nuelltiez az yoong girls
" that

"that had never feen Coourt afore."
Then did the men of Coventree make
petition that they "moought renue now
"their old Storical Sheaw,"—"of late
"laid doouu they knoe no cawz why,
"onlefs it wear by the zeal of certain
"theyr preacherz. Men very commend-
"able for their behaviour and learning,
"and fweet in their fermons, but fome-
"what too four in preaching awey theyr
"Paftime."*

Among the young girls who had never
feen Court afore we may probably reckon
Joyce Clopton, for the author has difcovered, among the pedigree MSS. in his
cuftody, that at an early age Joyce was
appointed

---

* A curious MS. copy of the celebrated "Letter
"wherein part of the Entertainment unto the Queen'z
"Majefty at Killingwoorth Caftl: in Warwickfheer in
"this Soomerz Progreft, 1575, is fignified," is in the
author's poffeffion. The writer notes "this manufcript
"is valuable." The author's name is given, Langham.
Mr. Knight calls him "the entertaining coxcomb,
"Laneham."

Stratford-upon-Avon. 165

appointed a Maid of Honour to Queen Elizabeth, being "a great favourite and "remarkable for her virtues." Moſt likely the Queen firſt ſaw the little girl, aged ſeven, on this memorable occaſion, when William Clopton (C), her father, came to Kenilworth to do honour to Leiceſter. However this may be, the lithe Joyce muſt have been brought about the Queen's perſon at a very youthful period, for young George Carew, a Captain in the army, met her, made love to her, and married her without her father's knowledge when ſhe was 19 years of age!
" Mr. Clopton was greatly diſpleaſed
" with his daughter's marriage with Cap-
" tain Carew, which was without his
" knowledge and conſent, and intended to
" diſinherit her. But upon an accidental
" meeting and converſing with Captain
" Carew, he found him a man of ſuperior
" genius and fine addreſs, which quali-
" fications

"fications so effectually recommended him to his favour that he was reconciled, and settled his estate at Clopton, which was very considerable, upon him and his daughter."

By reference to the Pedigree, it will be found that Clopton House was in the possession of three persons during the whole of Shakespere's life. William Clopton (C) inherited it three years before the Poet's birth, and enjoyed it until 1592, when Shakespere was 28 years of age. Joyce and her husband succeeded, and long outlived the Poet.

In these three persons we have individuals of rank, importance, and intellectual power. The traditions which associate Shakespere with Clopton House would be of little value, were it not that they are finger-posts directing us to inquiries which give us every confidence that he was so associated. The Combes, Cloptons,

Cloptons, Underhills, Boughtons (of Lawford), we find linked together by family ties and focial bonds. In the midft of them, in the " Great Houfe," that had belonged to the families of two of them, Shakefpere refided. It is a happy, pleafant picture that the mind creates for itfelf, as in imagination it repeoples the College, and New Place, and Clopton Houfe, and the neighbouring refidences of Idlicote and Boughton. We feem to fee our Shakefpere enjoying, and enjoyed in, fuch fociety. When we turn to the Pedigree, and learn what was the character and fame of George Carew, Earl of Totnefs, we can conceive in the brave foldier's periods of leave and repofe how greatly he would appreciate fuch converfation as he might find in New Place. Carew was himfelf an author, and efteemed a literary character in his day. Being fent by James I., in 1609, on an embaffy to to France, he drew up on his return a relation of the ſtate of that country, and gave portraitures of Henri Quatre, and of the principal people about the Court. He alſo wrote the "*Pacata Hibernia*," a hiſtory of the wars in Ireland, which Biſhop Nicholſon ſays contained the tranſactions of three years of much fighting, in Munſter, from the latter end of the year 1599 to the death of Queen Elizabeth. He alſo tranſlated into Engliſh a hiſtory of Iriſh affairs, written by Maurice Regan, a ſervant of the King of Leinſter, in the year 1171; the MS. of which work was formerly in the library of the Duke of Chandos.

Without purſuing the records of pedigrees further, it is to be hoped that enough has been brought forward to anſwer the queſtion at page 105, which the author ſuppoſed being put to him.

It is true there is no poſitive and direct evidence

evidence that Shakefpere ever affociated with many of the perfons that have been named. Heaven forbid that there ever fhould be found any direct evidence that he affociated with any of the perfons into whofe fociety he is degraded by tradition!

But which is the truftier of the two— the fair and natural conclufions which the mind draws from the contemplation of contemporaneous facts; or the idle, loofe, and fhifting ftories of perfons who had never feen the Poet, or could fpeak a word from their own knowledge?

Shakefpere's character, read by the offenfive taper-light of village goffip, is not the character which the ftudent of his works would expect to meet, and be miferably difappointed if he did not meet.

The weights and meafures of confcience—the things fhe approves, or difapproves—have one eternal, unchanging ftandard. In every age there is the fame fenfe sense of right and wrong, clean and unclean, sober and dissolute. Shakespere either was or was not a man to love and respect, as well as a Poet to admire. If he sank so low as to have his pastime with tipplers and drunkards, then our diminished regard tarnishes the brilliancy of our admiration. But if there is absolutely no evidence whatever to prove aught against the man; if deer stealing, and vagabondising, and hard drinking are unsupported by a single established, proved fact; and if, on the contrary, they are singularly at variance with what *are the known facts* of this great man's life, it is but just to his memory, and giving him the honour which is his due, if we scout with contempt the wrencings of tap-tubs and the vulgar gossip of clowns.

The view of Shakespere's life and character which the writer takes, is not drawn from imagination, presenting

ing an outline which will admit of no faults. It is eafy to mount a Pegafus, and foar aloft on the wings of grandiloquent words about his genius, and his poetry, and his dramatic fkill. It is the profaic, and not the fentimental, view of the man Shakefpere with which thefe pages are engaged. It is Shakefpere's Home which is their concern. Planting our feet on a few acres of land, under the fhadow of Holy Crofs, in Stratford, the object is to know as much as poffible about that home hiftorically and focially, and to know what the man was who inhabited it.

His ambition to acquire poffeffion of New Place was as honourable and laudable as it feems natural. Was not John Shakefpere, the Poet's father, engaged in the fame trade as the great Sir Hugh Clopton, however wide the difference in the extent of their dealings? That Great Houfe

House had been the London mercer's home. It had belonged to the man who made his money in Old Jewry and the Cheape. Before Shakespere set out for London, when his father was in difficulties, he very probably took a lingering look at the house,—took courage from the memory of the man who had lived in it,—and set out for London town with a stern determination to win independence himself, and return to live in Stratford, enjoying it. Let us review the circumstances of his life, and we shall find all this is most natural, and harmonises with what we know *are facts*. His running away to London, like a thief, to escape Sir Thomas Lucy, is a wretched, crack-brained story, based upon no fact whatever; but invented solely to try and make out a reason for Shakespere's going, when a natural and sufficient reason laid close at hand.

Lord

Lord Southampton gave him £1000 to complete fome purchafe he greatly defired. There was a purchafe completed, and probably completed in a hurry, for the vendor fold in Eafter term, and was dead in July! May not Lord Southampton's money have been given for this particular purpofe? And when Shakefpere was fettled at New Place, what are the evidences, the *facts*, we know of him? They uniformly go to prove that he was a careful, induftrious, money-making man, feeking to acquire property and to found a family. His proper ambition is difcoverable in every movement of his life: in his acquirement of New Place; in his grant of arms by the College; in his will; in his various purchafes of property; and, laft of all, in the fociety of the perfons with whom we conclude, both by pofitive and alfo by indirect evidence, that he affociated.

As

As we tread the garden of New Place, and recall the mighty dead that once trod that fame plot of earth, and called it his, let thofe who love to think of him as the Poet, think of him alfo as the Gentleman. The idle talk of men who never knew him has wafted down to us unproved and difcreditable ftories. At his threfhold, when we enter New Place, let us fhake them, with the duft, from off our feet. Shakefpere's honeft, anxious life deferves better from us than a readinefs to hear him defamed. As we tread his garden let us think of him, and judge of him *by what we know of him.* It is not much, indeed, but it may fome day be more. Such evidence as we have, all tells in his favour. It prefents to us a man with goodly ambition raifing himfelf and his family to prefent independence, and to everlafting fame. It prefents to us a cautious, careful labourer—

a painftaking artift, a moft fkilful anatomift of human nature. It prefents to us no hurried fcribbler of plays, careleffly throwing off, without an idea of their beauty, the teeming imaginations of his brain, as it has been impudently afferted; but a man who chaftened his mufe with fevere caftigation, and applied himfelf through life with unhalting felf-devotion, not only to feek out the treafures of thought, but to polifh, and fet his gems in fuch marvellous frameworks of plot, as in *Othello*, *Lear*, *Hamlet*, and *Macbeth*, that the world has gazed thefe three hundred years with admiration and delight upon his wondrous workmanfhip.

And when we tread his garden let us think of him as the greateft, loftieft teacher of mankind who has ever fpoken with uninfpired lips. "There are," faid Watfon, Bifhop of Llandaff (to the late Duke of Rutland, when retiring from his tutorfhip), tutorſhip), "two books to adhere to in "your future life; one is the Book of the "Child of God; the other the Book of "the Child of Nature."

From Shakeſpere's House at New Place, many of the pages of that book went forth to the world; and in that garden, among its trees and flowers, their thoughts were meditated. Let us honour his memory where his very preſence ſeems to overſhadow us.

> *" A gleam of daylight ſet*
> *Will gild the cloud of eve ;*
> *And the ſoul's light linger yet*
> *O'er the place it ſighed to leave."*

In writing about Shakeſpere, inches of faƈt have been fringed with acres of conjeƈture. When once an author has entered upon the field of conjeƈture he can wander along at his will, unchecked and

and unhindered! But if conjecture is fuggeftive of inquiry, where inquiry may not have been fufficiently made, perhaps it is not altogether worthlefs.

Where did Shakefpere obtain his knowledge? That queftion has been afked by every ftudent of his works, and has never yet been fatisfactorily anfwered.

Ben Jonfon afferted that he had "fmall Latine, and leffe Greeke," by which, it is to be prefumed, he meant to ftate that Shakefpere had received the rudiments of a claffical education, without being diftinguifhed as a fcholar. Such a conclufion might be fairly arrived at from a ftudy of his plays. But though he might not have been able to tranflate the Medea or Antigone with eafe, it does not admit of a doubt, that in fome way or other, and at an early age, he muft have read extenfively — perhaps indifcriminately.

At

At eighteen he married. The youth, whether he was a lawyer's clerk, or apprenticed to bufinefs, had finifhed his curriculum at fchool before that event. We are confequently reduced to the neceffity of confidering his " education " (technically fo called) as finifhed when he was feventeen years of age. Had he acquired the mafs of information with which his mind was ftored, previous to that date? or, during the labours of author and actor in London, did he find time to purfue the cultivation of his mind, as well as to inform himfelf of the data and hiftorical facts regarding any particular play which he was going to write? A diftinguifhed magiftrate of the prefent day once anfwered the writer of thefe lines (on his expreffing furprife at the minutely accurate information difplayed by a popular novelift regarding the local hiftory and hiftorical records of a place he
had

had never visited), "Oh! give a man a "fortnight at the British Museum and he "will get up any period or place you "please." No doubt there is much truth in this remark; but, *imprimis*, Shakespere had no British Museum to which he could refer; and, in the next place, the knowledge he displays in *Romeo*, *Hamlet*, *Macbeth*, or any of the plays, the plots of which he borrowed from historical books, tracts, or stories he had read, is of a very much deeper and profounder character, than results from cursory reading. It is not the knowledge of a "common-place "book," or a "cram," but the result of keen observation and close study.

Not in the technical, but in the broadest sense of the term "education," insufficient inquiry has been made, as to how, or by what means, Shakespere became self-educated? for it does not admit of dispute that his profound knowledge of
human

human nature, and his marvellous capacity for the acquiſition of facts, were the reſult of ſelf-cultivation. No grammar ſchool of King Edward VI. inſtructed a boy's mind as Shakeſpere's mind was inſtructed.

Conjecture ſpeculates as to how he gained his information?

Suggeſtion, with a ſurmiſe, may inquire whether the hiſtory of the "Guild" at Stratford has ever been narrowly ſcrutiniſed, with a view to arriving at a concluſion.

Shakeſpere's lines in the Third Act of the *Twelfth Night* have been repeatedly quoted:—

> MARIA. *He's in yellow ſtockings.*
> SIR TOBY. *And croſs-gartered.*
> MARIA. *Moſt villainouſly; like a pedant that keeps a ſchool i' the church.*

Whether Shakeſpere had his own preceptor before his mind's eye, may be doubted; but there can be no doubt that he he alludes to a cuſtom of his time, which had come under his own obſervation, which was the very common habit of holding public ſchools in the Lady chapels, or chancels of churches which had formerly been connected with monaſtic eſtabliſhments.

There are many perſons alive who have belonged to ſchools kept in the church—as, for inſtance, the Queen Elizabeth School, which was held in the Lady chapel of St. Mary Redcliffe at Briſtol, and in which they received their education. Schools in the church were not uncommon. The ſchool at St. Alban's continues to be held in the Lady chapel of that ſtupendous Norman abbey, to the preſent hour. A ſchool was kept (perhaps ſtill is) in the Triforium of Chriſt Church, Hants. The college ſchool at Worceſter alſo has been held in a noble hall within the Cathedral precincts. A long liſt of ſuch ſchools in the church might

might be given. But there is one remarkable fact connected with them; they have, as a general rule, been established or held in the Lady chapels, or chapels of suppressed monastic institutions, and not in buildings that were parochial churches before the Reformation. In connection with these suppressed monasteries, or cells, there were frequently valuable libraries, rich in ancient chronicles, tales of the wars, histories of royal heroes and valiant knights, as well as in the lives of the saints, missals, and breviaries.

Such an establishment was the Guild of the Holy Cross. Henry VIII. suppressed its conventual character. His son Edward VI. erected it into a grammar school. The Corporation records of Stratford prove that the chancel of the Guild Chapel was used as a " school i' the church," and it is altogether uncertain whether such use was continuous or temporary. Mr. Halliwell

Stratford-upon-Avon. 183

well and others imagine it was temporary, founding their opinions upon probabilities as they suggest themselves to their minds from an examination of the Corporation books. The items of allowances there alluded to in 1568 are:—" for repayryng " the scole;" " for dressyng and sweepyng " the scole house;" " for ground and " sellynge in the olde scole;" " for takyng " doun the soller over the scole." Mr. Halliwell comments upon this—" This " last entry would alone seem to prove " that the school was not then in the " chapel, but in another building."

The difference in the terms of designation seems to warrant the opinion that there may have been an intended distinction between the " scole" and " olde " scole." The use of the word " olde " appears to signify that there were two school-rooms, or places of teaching, belonging to the one " Grammar School,"
answering

answering probably to what is called in the present day, the upper and lower school. And if the chancel of the Guild Chapel had lately been appropriated for scholastic purposes, it was very natural in the Chamberlain's accounts, to describe the school-room in the monastic buildings of the ancient guild as " the " olde scole." It was the truest description, for the same place had been " a " scole " for fifty-two years previous to the suppression of the monasteries, having been founded in the last year of the reign of Edward IV., 1482, by a Thomas Jolyffe, under charge and control of the Guild of the Holy Cross.

There is another entry and date in the Corporation books, of great importance. In February, 1594, an order directs, that there shall be no school kept in the chapel from that date. It will be fair to conclude, that up to that year, from the new

new foundation of the school in the 7th year of the reign of Edward VI., 1553, the Guild Chapel had been used for school-teaching; and in all probability about that date, the "olde scole" had such additional accommodation given to it, that it was no longer necessary to appropriate the Guild Chapel to such a purpose. Whether it was habitually used as a school from 1554 to 1594 (as the Lady chapel of St. Alban's still is, and St. Mary Redcliffe was until lately), is of no great moment, because distinct evidence proves, that, whether occasionally or habitually, to such use it was devoted during the years when Shakespere was at school, and (supposing he continued at school until he was sixteen) for fourteen years subsequently.

It may yet be discovered that greater impressions were produced upon the mind of the boy Shakespere by the advantages

tages he derived from the "school i' the "church," than have ever been suggested by commentators upon his life! Many obscurities have of late years been cleared up, by a careful perusal of documents hitherto neglected.

There are possibly in existence many documents, which, if discovered, would throw a flood of light upon the business of his manhood and his authorship, that remain for the present shrouded in obscurity. Probably enough, on that night in June, 1613, when Burbage was performing *Henry VIII.* in the Globe Theatre, Blackfriars, and the thatched roof catching fire, the entire building was destroyed, many MSS., plays, and note-books of the Poet's, may have perished in the flames, which would have set at rest the unsatisfactory question—How did Shakespere acquire his varied, profound, and also desultory knowledge?

The

The inquiry seems to force us to one or other of two conclusions: either he enjoyed peculiar advantages from the "school i' the church" which could not be derived from the ordinary cross-gartered pedants' routine of *Hic, Hæc, Hoc*, or he must have been enabled, by Lord Southampton, or some other influential person, to obtain access to a library in London. At the present moment, in the utter absence of all direct evidence upon the subject, we are thrown back upon probabilities, and the indirect internal evidence of Shakespere's writings. They appear to bear a twofold witness in favour both of Stratford and London; but such knowledge as so busy a man could acquire in London, was much more likely to be obtained for the occasion, and studied in histories and chronicles hurriedly, in order to construct the plots of his pieces, than to be of that profound and equally discursive

curſive character, which remains to the preſent time the admiration and equally the puzzle of the world. In the plays which we know that Shakeſpere wrote, when one of the " owners " or " partners " of the Globe Theatre, and in the full ſtrain of mental and phyſical exertion, we do find an immenſe amount of that "knowledge of a period" before alluded to, which is rather the buſineſs of a ſearcher of records, than of a ſtudent of literature. This, after all, is the mere ſkeleton of a play. The fleſh and life that clothe thoſe dry bones of history, could not be ſo read-up or crammed. The plays of *Henry IV.* and *Henry VI.* may ſerve for example. No Garter-King-at-Arms, no F.S.A. could ſupply us with more accurate knowledge of deſcent and pedigree, than do ſuch ſpeeches as thoſe of Mortimer (Firſt Part *Henry VI.*, Act ii.), and of the Duke of York (Second Part

Part *Henry VI.*, Act ii.). No historian could sketch character more admirably, or render narrative more transparent, than do the princes and prelates who speak in Act iv. Second Part of *Henry IV.* But while such knowledge might have been studied for the purpose, let it be remembered that this same Act is world-famous for a knowledge of a very different character—a knowledge of human nature, exhibited in the two phases of high and ordinary life,—King Henry and the Prince; and Justice Shallow, Falstaff, and Bardolph,—in itself sufficient to have established the fame of a humorist or satirist of any age. It is not a question of probability, but a known fact, that Shakespere did model the skeletons of many of his plays upon the chronicles which he read while actively occupied at the Globe Theatre. Still, that does not account for the flesh, and blood, and life, with which

which they are quickened; and in order to do so, it seems necessary to retrace our steps to Stratford, and to attribute them to a precocious acquisitiveness, as well as natural quickness of observation. Quickness of observation seems necessarily allied with the keenest sense of the ludicrous. The *traditions* of Stratford concerning the Poet's humour, *may well be trusted when we read his plays;* and when we regard him as a satirist of the follies of mankind, in comparison with the satirists of modern times, their attacks are but as the prick of a bodkin or a pin, compared with the flaying of a scalping-knife!

Shakespere's knowledge was two-fold: it was the most wonderful that any human being has ever exhibited, regarded as knowledge resulting from observation; but it was also knowledge acquired by reading and study. In him every one recognises

nises the student as well as the observer. When did he study? Where did he study? A great amount of his knowledge of life, as exhibited in his rustic characters and clowns, was, we know, the photographing of persons with whom he had come in contact in Warwickshire! There also most probably was his study! It has been asserted that, towards the close of his life, he regularly retired to Stratford for the purpose of writing his plays. The assertion carries with it every probability, and it is likely enough the truth, that at Stratford he was habitually a student to the very close of his career. If the *Tempest* or *Henry VIII.* were the last plays he wrote, he must have been such. We may well incline to the belief, when we remember the touching farewells of Prospero and Wolsey to that power which they had so long exercised. Shakespere himself might be speaking

to

to us in the "long farewell," or in the lines:—

> *"I'll break my staff,*
> *Bury it certain fathoms in the earth,*
> *And deeper than did ever plummet found,*
> *I'll drown my book."*

It is not, however, with the close but with the commencement of his career, that we have to do. Was not Stratford the school-house of his life? Did not his mind,— with a precocity such as has been exhibited in Milton and Chatterton, and for which Lord Byron was nervously anxious that the world should give him credit,—eagerly and thirstily drink at the sources of such knowledge as were capable of being reached in his youthful years? Though it may seemingly be a very unsatisfactory manner of answering a question, to put another; nevertheless, when every lover of Shakespere has asked, and will continue to ask until the question is answered, "Where did the Poet gain his
"diversified

"diverſified learning?" it may not be altogether uſeleſs to reply to ſuch inquirers—Have you not paſſed over, without ſufficiently ſearching conſideration, the days that were ſpent at "the ſchool i' the "church?" Have you thoroughly inveſtigated the character of that ſchool, and of the Guild of the Holy Croſs, with which it was originally incorporated? Have you ſatisfied yourſelves, whether, in that very church, Shakeſpere might not have found thoſe ſources of knowledge which he evidently found ſomewhere and ſomehow?

Between the date when King Henry VIII. ſuppreſſed the monaſtic eſtabliſhment in 1536, to the date of his ſon, Edward VI., reviving the School of the Guild in 1553, only ſeventeen years intervened. Thoſe years were long enough to complete the work of diſperſion or deſtruction among the libraries of abbeys that

that were themselves reduced to ruins, but no such ruin overtook the Guild of the Holy Cross. It was not an establishment of sufficient importance to be ruined, and accordingly it changed hands, and followed the destinies of the Reformation.

What became of its furniture—its chattels—above all, its books? Was there any library connected with the Free School of the Guild? If so, what object could there be for the officers of Henry VIII. to destroy it, or disperse it?

The problem as to where Shakespere gained his extensive knowledge, can never be solved until inquiries in this direction shall be—if ever—satisfactorily answered. The ground, to the best belief of the author, is almost, if not altogether, unbroken ground. Whether the readers of these pages will feel the same conviction that he does, it is not for him

him to know; but, while the moſt intereſting of all inquiries regarding the life of Shakeſpere ſtill waits for an anſwer, the author has convinced himſelf, that if that anſwer is ever rendered, it will come from Stratford, and not from London;—it will prove that William Shakeſpere, while a ſchool-boy, with little Latin and leſs Greek, had neverthelefs a thirſt for knowledge in his own mother-tongue, a love for acquiring information of the moſt diverſified character, and a marvellous power, or natural gift, for *hiving* his ſtore in the cells of memory, and bringing forth that knowledge, "ſweeter than honey or "the honeycomb," whenever it was required. With a conviction, which nothing but abſolute evidence to the contrary would ever ſhake, the author feels morally certain that at the "ſchool i' the church" Shakeſpere had free acceſs to ſome valuable ſtore of books, whether belonging

to

to the Guild proper, or to the school of the Guild, or to some other library that was contiguous and easily accessible; and that from the same sources at which the thirsting school-boy drank, the man, in his occasional and eventually permanent retirement, drank also. Perhaps there may have been a peculiar charm and attraction for this teacher of mankind in settling at New Place, because its gables and casements were shadowed by the glorious architecture of that Holy Cross Chapel, wherein he had discovered, and ever after fondly sought, those silent teachers—dear and precious books!—the unquarrelling friends, the unchanging companions, the charmers whose charms never fade;—alike welcome to the man in the zenith of literary fame, and to the school-boy with satchel and shining morning face, eagerly seeking (as King Edward named the master of the Stratford School)

School) the Pedagogue and "the fchool "i' the church."

Though the remains are very fcanty that ferve to give us any information regarding Shakefpere, it is fomewhat remarkable that one of the moft valuable relics connected with him fhould have belonged to his library. One book of Shakefpere's, with his autograph on the fly-leaf, exifts. It is Montaigne's Effays. Amidft the goffip of literature with which the modern Prefs abounds, it is no fmall teftimony to the worth of fuch books as Montaigne's Effays, and Burton's Anatomy of Melancholy, that they ftand without rivals to the prefent hour; approached only by Hallam, by D'Ifraeli's "Curiofities of Literature," and one or two other works of like character, but unfurpaffed by any, in their own quaint

quaint and captivating style of historical anecdote.

That Montaigne should be a favourite author with Shakespere will be readily understood by any one who has studied the minds of the two men. They were both satirists of the eccentricities of human nature. They had both a relish for conceits. They were both philosophers of life. We can well imagine that Montaigne would be as valued on the shelves of New Place, as Charles Lamb describes a new book to have been valued, when it was at last acquired after the careful storing of every spare farthing, and carried home in triumph to his sister!

Shakespere's one book! And such a book! What more humorous, instructive, entertaining, and improving companion could a man need than Montaigne's Essays? Leaving to Mr. Emerson

Emerson and Mr. St. John the task of apologising for the occasionally eccentric tendency of the Gascon's fancy—remembering the fashion of the times in which he lived, and the vernacular even of courts and kings, which in modern days would make the hair of society stand on end—we might be permitted to arrange in imagination the bookshelves of New Place, and with the single vertebra of a library—Montaigne's Essays—proceed to the formation of the body of Shakespere's fireside literature, as Professor Owen constructs an animal upon the authority of a bone. Astonishing as the number of works is which Caxton contrived to produce between the publication of the " Game of "Chess," in 1474, and his death in 1491—*the year before Sir Hugh Clopton was Lord Mayor of London*—equalling as much as five thousand closely printed folio pages, this leaping of the giant in the womb of time

time (as Mr. Hallam called it) was nothing in comparifon with the production of books during the feventy years that intervened between the date of Caxton's death and Shakefpere's birth. The great printer's favourite apprentices, Pynfon and Wynkyn de Worde, had between them publifhed more than fix hundred volumes at the end of the firft quarter of the fixteenth century. When once the preffes had been eftablifhed at Oxford and other large provincial towns, the iffue averaged feventy-five volumes a year. So that, by the clofe of the century when Shakefpere modelled and furnifhed his houfe at New Place, he had the pick of ten thoufand volumes publifhed in the Englifh tongue, and could adorn his ftudy either with Cranmer's Bible, publifhed by Grafton, or with one of John Day's; or with that edition of 1551 for which Tindall was ftrangled, and his body burnt. In
addition

addition to this, the retirement of Stratford would be enlivened for him by the arrival of "Mercuries" or "Flying "Couriers," in which the lateſt intelligence from Town would be recorded, and he might fee what Heminge and Burbage were about at the Globe.

When ſpeculations are hazarded as to the knowledge of Shakeſpere, and its ſources, it is defirable to have facts of this defcription recalled to mind. We ordinarily labour under the impreffion that books were very ſcarce in Shakeſpere's days; and if we may take Lord Macaulay's celebrated picture of England's country houſes in the time of Charles II. as something like the truth, we may make a pretty fair gueſs at what would be the amount of intellectual food enjoyed by the gentry and ſquires of Warwickſhire juſt one century earlier. If, between 1660 and 1665, " the difficulty and ex-
" penſe

"penfe of carrying large packets from
"place to place was fo great that an ex-
"tenfive work was longer in making its
"way from Paternofter Row to Devon-
"fhire or Lancafhire than it now is in
"reaching Kentucky," .... and "few
"Knights of the Shire had libraries fo
"good as may now perpetually be found
"in a fervants' hall," the fubject of rural
intellectuality would be depreffing indeed, on glancing backwards one hundred
years prior to fuch Bœotian darknefs, were
it not that the crab-like movement in this
inftance would be pofitive progrefs, fince
there can be no queftion that learning
degraded in England between the dates
1560 and 1660.

Upon Shakefpere's claffical knowledge,
or maftery of languages, there is little to
be faid, or that needs to be faid fince the
publication of Dr. Farmer's (the Mafter
of Emmanuel College, Cambridge,)
"Effay

"Eſſay on the Learning of Shakeſpere." That exhauſtive pamphlet, Malone candidly admitted, was overwhelming in its evidence, and concluſive, that the Poet's claſſical plays and poems were not conſtructed upon a knowledge of the claſſic authors, but upon tranſlations of thoſe authors. Whether Ben Jonſon ever uttered the ſlighting words attributed to him or not, he would be a rampant enthuſiaſt indeed who would dare to contravene the truth of the words themſelves. Nothing can be more concluſive of Shakeſpere's mere ſchoolboy knowledge of Latin than his abſurd miſquotation from Lily's Grammar of a line which, for the purpoſe of example, is given one way in the grammar, but runs very differently in the " Eunu-" chus " of Terence, from which, had our Poet really been quoting, he would have quoted correctly. In the

the *Taming of the Shrew*, we read (Act i. Scene 1)—

> TRANIO. *Mafter, it is no time to chide you now;*
> *Affection is not rated from the heart:*
> *If love have touch'd you, naught remains but fo,—*
> *" Redime te captum quam queas minimo."*

In the original ("Eunuchus," I. i. 29) the paffage ftands thus:—

> PHŒDRIA. *Nec quid agam, fcio.*
> PARMENO. *Quid agas? Nifi ut te redimas captum quam queas*
> *Minimo: fi nequeas paululo, at quanti queas*
> *Et ne te afflictes.*
> PHŒDRIA. *Itane fuades, &c., &c.*

The truth was that Shakefpere had learnt Lily's Grammar at fchool (with its "Epiftle" and directions by Cardinal Wolfey).

We have no poffible reafon for fuppofing that he ever pretended to fcholarfhip. He put into the mouth of Tranio a line with which, in his day, every fchoolboy was familiar; but from whence derived,

derived, it is very probable, Shakefpere neither knew nor cared. Probably, with his keen humour, no one could have enjoyed a laugh more than he, could he have liftened to the rubbifh which Shakefperian " fcholars " have talked about the claffical knowledge of a man who was too honeft even to pretend to any familiarity with the Greek and Latin poets.

The well-worn ftory of Mr. Hales, of Eton, filtering through the works of Rowe, Dryden, and Gilrow, is equally honourable to Mr. Hales, and probably clofe to the truth.

Rowe writes: " In a converfation be-
" tween Sir John Suckling, Sir William
" D'Avenant, Endymion Porter, Mr.
" Hales, of Eton, and Ben Jonfon, Sir
" John Suckling, who was a profeffed
" admirer of Shakefpere, had undertaken
" his defence againft Ben Jonfon with
" fome warmth; Mr. Hales, who had
" fat

" sat still for some time told them,
" '*That if Mr. Shakspeare had not read*
" '*the ancients, he had likewise not stolen*
" '*anything from them; and that if he*
" '*would produce any one topick finely*
" '*treated by any one of them, he would*
" '*undertake to show something upon the*
" '*same subject at least as well written by*
" '*Shakspeare.*' "

Fifteen years before Rowe's Life of Shakespere had been published, Gildon's Letters and Essays (in 1694) told the story. "The enemies of Shakespere
" would by no means yield him so much
" excellence: so that it came to a reso-
" lution of a trial of skill upon that sub-
" ject. The place agreed on for the dis-
" pute was Mr. Hale's chamber at Eton.
" A great many books were sent down by
" the enemies of this Poet; and on the
" appointed day, my Lord Falkland, Sir
" John Suckling, and all the persons of
" quality

"quality that had wit and learning, and
"interested themselves in the quarrel,
"met there; and, upon a thorough dif-
"quisition of the point, the judges,
"chosen by agreement out of this learned
"and ingenious assembly, unanimously
"gave the preference to Shakspeare,
"and the Greek and Roman poets were
"adjudged to vail at least their glory in
"that to the English hero."

Dryden's allusion to the story ("Essay
"on Dramatic Poesy," 1667,) is as follows: "The consideration of this made
"Mr. Hales, of Eton, say, ' that there
"' was no subject of which any poet ever
"' writ, but he would produce it much
"' better done by Shakspeare.'"

The "ever-memorable" John Hales
was a scholar of distinguished European
reputation, and, therefore, he must have
been as familiar with the Greek and Latin
poets as with Shakespere. He was one
of

of those ripe and broadly read scholars—
not thick as blackberries even in the nineteenth century—who are as familiar with
the poetry of their own country as with
that of the ancients. History has assured
us of this: and how very few there are
like him! How very few those who
can " cap verses " in that highest range
of literary knowledge, where Terence,
Horace, Sophocles, and Euripides, can be
instantly answered by the quotation of a
kindred line from Spenser, Shakespere, or
Milton. Hales was one of these few
athletes of scholarship, and therefore his
opinion is worthy of all consideration,
while his celebrated victory deserves to
make him, as Malone prayed he might
remain, " ever-memorable."

The mental gymnastics thus performed
in Mr. Hale's room at Eton, seem to
point out very distinctly the strength and
the weakness of Shakespere! " If he
" had

"had not read the ancients!" What then? Mr. Hales knew he had not. Deeply read himfelf in the claffics, he knew that his favourite was not fo. But, what then? Point out any moral, any philofophic reflection, any noble and elevating fentiment, produced by the ancient poets, and "I will produce it "much better done by Shakfpeare," faid Mr. Hales.

From the crucible to which Dr. Farmer fubjected the writings of Shakefpere, they came forth purged from that alloy of filly eulogy which was a drofs, giving to the Poet what never belonged to him, and depreciating the pure coinage uttered by his brilliant brain. The marvel of Shakefpere's works is in the beauties that are all his own. The prodigality of his genius may in fome degree be eftimated when one of England's greateft fcholars challenges the ancient poets, and declares
himfelf

himself ready to "cap" any sentiment of their verse by a similar sentiment, equally well or better expressed in Shakespere. And who, in the trial, wins the victory? Let it be granted frankly that Shakespere, in writing his *Troilus and Cressida*, followed Caxton's History of Troy; that he borrowed from Plutarch; that he read Hollinshed in order to construct *Richard III.*; that he studied a translation of Belleforest before he wrote *Hamlet!* — Let the same sort of facts be quoted against *Henry IV.*, *Richard II.*, and all the historical plays: and what does it amount to? Both the closet and the stage are witnesses to the truth, that the more "historical" the Poet is — the more he depends upon and adheres to chronicles or legends—the less powerful he is. Those plays are the least popular which are the most historical, for the simple reason that

that where he has to trace the history of a reign in the cramped limits of a play, he is necessarily fettered, and the scope of the Poet's fancy is more or less subjected to the inevitable rehearsal of facts. How different is it in the unapproached perfection of treatment, progressive development of plot, and poetry of diction in *Othello* and *Macbeth*. In those, as in *Hamlet*, and *Romeo*, and *King Lear*, a scheme of the play has been derived from ancient writers, or translations, but nothing more. The genius of the Poet has been left free to portray character, and to clothe sentiment with words as no other poet ever did.

There is every difference between learning and language. Shakespere's knowledge was not a knowledge of language, but it was the knowledge of learning. It is highly probable that he never derived a single classical incident, allusion, or

story

story, direct from a classical author. It is equally probable that he never in his life read a Greek play, and knew no more of Terence than he had learnt of him in Lily's Grammar!

The more we realise these facts (for they are facts), and the more surprising the learning of the Poet becomes, he does not thereby sink, but rather rises in our admiration. We strip him of pretensions—*post-mortem* honours to which he laid no claim—and regard him solely as what he is, the Poet of England, and uttering in English verse the thoughts gathered from, or suggested by, English literature.

We have seen that there were ten thousand volumes published in English during the century in which he flourished, and that every year contributed largely to the information of studious men. Whatever truth there may be in
Macaulay's

Macaulay's strictures upon the ignorance prevailing in the reign of Charles II., the business of Shakespere's life involved reading and study. And although it is true that the circulation of books in the rural districts of England may have been very slow, still this objection would not be any impediment to Shakespere, who, living constantly in London, and travelling to and fro between Stratford and town, would have ample opportunity to take down with him into the country any books which he wished to read. Chronological tables of the order in which his plays were written, founded upon internal evidence, dates of performance, or of publication, have frequently been published. Such tables are after all conjectural, and it is no proof of the date when a play was written, to learn when it was printed or played. In the absence of demonstration, the conjectures of
Malone

Malone and Chalmers attribute, the one seven, the other eleven plays to Shakespere prior to his purchase of New Place in 1597. The far more satisfactory, because positive, facts which Mr. C. Knight gives us, show that only three plays had been published prior to 1597. With a very trifling amount of exception it may, therefore, be stated that the mass of his plays were written during his tenancy of New Place; and all the greatest, without doubt, during the latter period of his life. Within sixteen years thirty-four plays of Shakespere's were either printed or spoken of in print, giving us an average of two plays a year; their actual publication, or direct allusion to them in particular years, being as follows:—

In 1597	3 Plays.
,, 1598	8 ,,
,, 1600	5 ,,
,, 1602	3 ,,

In

In 1603 . . . . 1 Play.
„ 1604 . . . . 1 „
„ 1607 . . . . 2 „
„ 1609 . . . . 2 „
„ 1611 . . . . 2 „
„ 1613 . . . . 1 „

It is very remarkable that, according to this lift, the Poet worked the hardeft during the year he became poffeffed of New Place, and for the four or five years fubfequent. It feems natural to conclude that Shakefpere purchafed New Place with a view to making it his literary fanctum; for it is impoffible to refift connecting with the purchafe, the fecundity of his pen. Let us only confider the character of work in which he was employed when in London, and let any man fo engaged anfwer whether it would be poffible for Shakefpere, regularly employed at Blackfriars or the Globe, rehearfing and performing, to ftudy the plots and produce the MSS. of eight or five tragedies and comedies per annum. If he could have

have done so, he would have been a far greater prodigy than the world has ever yet accounted him. Such an Herculean labour of mind and body is beyond the capacity of any human being. But if we attach the purchase of New Place to Shakespere's success as a play-writer, and contemplate him withdrawing there from the excitement and bustle of Blackfriars to produce the *Merchant of Venice,* and *Midsummer Night's Dream,* then that garden, and the slender remains of the foundations of his house seem to become doubly precious to Englishmen. As time wears on his labours slacken; but almost to the end he continues bringing forth from the treasures of his mind the immortal works which gild his fame. The opinion of many writers has been that Shakespere was undomesticated, and that he rarely visited Stratford. Humbly, but confidently, the writer embraces a
directly

directly opposite opinion. To him it appears impossible that Shakespere could have accomplished the literary work he produced, immersed in the business and distracting engagements of Blackfriars or the Globe. Circumstances seem to give credit to the supposition that a larger amount of his time was spent at New Place than is commonly estimated; and as to his being undomesticated, or unhappy in his home, such an uncharitable and purely conjectural idea has not even as much respectability as the mare's-nest which De Quincey discovered in the marriage licence. The minds that give welcome to the one notion will, most likely, cherish the other.

Instead of Shakespere residing in London and occasionally visiting Stratford, it may be much nearer the truth to say that he lived the latter years of his life chiefly at New Place, and only visited London at those

those periods of the year when his presence was absolutely necessary. The probabilities are strongly in favour of this opinion, and there is no evidence to the contrary. For the last eighteen years of his life he is presented to our imagination as the master of New Place. He is not to be regarded during those years enjoying retirement and repose, like many of the great men who have followed him in his profession, as Garrick at Hampton, John Kemble at Lausanne, or Macready at Sherborne and Cheltenham.

The "silver livery of advised age," which it was permitted the two first—and long may it be allowed to the third—to wear, was never donned by Shakspere. He died in the freshness and vigour of life; and, as we know of a certainty, continued actively employed until the close of his existence. It is saddening to think how little associated with his private life
remains

remains to us. A letter, a will, a deed, a book—and that is all! How different the fate of the master and his apprentices. There are happily preserved to us the chief incidents in the life of Garrick; and many articles of personal property belonging to him, which are highly prized. When Shakespere was dead a hundred years, scarce a trace of him remained. A few stories gathered from gossips hung about his track in Stratford; but anything actually associated with him would have been as hard to discover there, as the Philosopher's Stone. The hundred years was only just completed, when the house in which he had lived and died was razed to the ground. The descendants of his sister, Joan Hart, as the pedigree shows, have reached down to our own days. Possibly some of them may still exist in the neighbourhood of Tewkesbury or Gloucester. To Joan he bequeathed not only

only his houfe in Henley Street, and twenty pounds, but alfo "all my wearing "apparel."

What would the world now give to fee a fuit of wearing apparel that had been worn by Shakefpere? If the coat of Napoleon in the Louvre, or of Nelfon in Greenwich Hofpital, attracts the attention of tens of thoufands, what would be the value of and intereft in the black gown, "garded with velvet and faced with "cony;" the ruddy coloured hofe, the caffock, the jerkin, the "fryze bryches," the rapier, and "the hat of a certain kind of "fine haire, fetched from beyond the feas, "which they call 'bever hatte.'"?*

Shakefpere's wardrobe muft have been ftocked with articles of this defcription. They were all left to his fifter; and his fifter's defcendants certainly furvived to the

---

* Fairholt's "Coftume in England," p. 216 (1860, Ed.)

the end of the laſt century. It would have ſeemed natural for them to have preſerved ſome of the coſtume of the Poet, but there is not a trace of anything of the ſort.

In the ſame way he bequeathed to Mr. Thomas Combe his ſword. The pedigree ſhows us how the Combe property paſſed into the Clopton family, by the marriage of Martha Combe with Edward Clopton. What would his countrymen not give to recover Shakeſpere's ſword? Its preſervation would have been moſt eaſy. If the ſword of the Conqueror could be preſerved in the family of the late Sir Godfrey Webſter, with the Roll of Battle, down to the middle of the laſt century, and only then periſhed through the misfortune of a fire, why could not the Combes and Cloptons have preſerved Shakeſpere's ſword? Why might it not have been depoſited ere this in in some national treasury? If there is an article of use which has the quality of defying accident and time, it is a sword. Very probably Shakespere's sword still exists, but has been lost or sold! Who knows whether it may not have been among the furniture and chattels sold off by Mr. Battersbee, previous to the demolition of Stratford College, the residence of the Combes?

What became of the broad silver-gilt bowl bequeathed to Judith Shakespere—Mrs. Quiney? What became of the "chattels, plate, jewels, and household "stuff" bequeathed to Dr. Hall and Mrs. Hall? These would naturally descend to Lady Barnard; and at her decease would continue in the use of Sir John Barnard, until his death in 1673. Neither Lady Barnard's will, nor the indenture relating to her property, make any mention of Shakespere's heir-looms. The
broad

broad filver-gilt bowl, the plate, the jewels, all vanifh from fight. Articles of this defcription do not perifh or confume away. They may exift now in as excellent prefervation as in 1616! If fo, what has become of them? Unlefs the filver bowl was fold by the Quineys, and melted down, it would moft probably be engraved with a creft, or a monogram, or fome device whereby it could be recognifed. Is it yet too late to inftitute a fearch for fuch an invaluable relic of the Poet? A man of Sir John Barnard's ftation would naturally leave plate, jewels, and property, to his heirs or relatives. It is faid that this family has died out within a very fhort time at *Abingdon, in Berkfhire*. If fuch is the fact, family heir-looms do not defcend to the grave: they pafs to fome one. If the inquiry has not yet been diligently made, it is well worth while to know in what direction

rection the Barnard property has gone; and to trace—failing direct male defcent—the female iffue, and the marriages which may have carried property into other families. It feems impoffible but that Elizabeth Hall muft have inherited the plate and jewels which belonged to her grandfather; and as fhe makes no direct mention of them in her will, it is natural to fuppofe they continued in poffeffion of her hufband.

We fee Shakefpere's perfonal property divided among his children and his fifter: to one his wardrobe is bequeathed, to another his plate, to another his broad filver bowl, and to Thomas Combe his fword! It is hard to believe that a man valued during his lifetime as Shakefpere was, and immortalifed fo quickly after his death, fhould be held in the leaft efteem by thofe of his own houfehold. It is hard to think that no one belonging to to him fhould defire to preferve the mementoes which he had particularly bequeathed to them in his will. And yet the fact ftares us in the face that not a fingle heir-loom of the Poet has been handed down, by any one branch of his family, to the prefent day! All, all are loft and gone, fave one book, the prefervation of which has been purely accidental!

Rowe, who acknowledges himfelf indebted to Betterton for a confiderable part of the paffages relating to the Poet's life introduced in his Biography (publifhed 1709), informs us that Betterton's "vener-
" ation for the memory of Shakefpere . . .
" engaged him to make a journey into
" Warwickfhire, on purpofe to gather
" up what remains he could of a name
" which he had in fo great veneration."
Confidering that Betterton was born in 1635—the fame year in which Dr. John

John Hall died—and that his daughter survived until 1669, when Betterton was thirty-four years of age,—and considering also that she was eight years of age when her grandfather died, and therefore perfectly able to speak of him from her own recollection,—it does seem extraordinary that the remains which Betterton went to Stratford to gather up were so scanty. He would find Shakespere's children all dead, but his residence in the possession of his grandchild, who, though living at Abington, was probably an occasional visitor to her property in Stratford. Had he even made her acquaintance, with what a fund of information might Rowe's Life have been enriched! and what treasures connected with the Poet might have been chronicled, and possibly preserved, through his interest! But the fates seem to have ordered it otherwise. The Poet had not been dead twenty years

years when Betterton was born; and within half a century of Shakefpere's deceafe, this venerator of his memory probably vifited Stratford. From that place he does not feem to have brought back with him a fingle memento of the Poet; or to have feen his fword, his filver bowl, his books, or any of his chattels, at a defcription of which the ears of every antiquary in England would now tingle, while to recover one of them would make any prefent difcoverer famous.

Fifty years, and the treafures of the Poet were unnoticed or unknown! One hundred years, and the domeftic affociations of his pupil and interpreter, David Garrick, are as frefhly and carefully preferved as if he had been in their midft yefterday! Within a mile of one another, at Hampton and Hampton Court, are two refidences, which,
fo

so long as they exift, will be for ever affociated with Shakefpere and Garrick. Thanks to Mr. Peter Cunningham's timely difcovery in the Audit Office of the "Revel's Booke," we now know when "Shaxberd's" *Plaie of Errors*, his *Marchant of Venis*, his *Mefur for Mefur*, and his *Merry Wives of Winfor*, were performed before James I. We know with certainty of two noble chambers — and thofe royal chambers—in which Shakefpere was feen and heard, and of none other; for though it would be almoft a profanity to difturb the tradition which identifies the houfe in Henley Street, Stratford, as the birthplace of the Poet, there is no abfolute certainty of fuch being the cafe. The Banqueting Houfe, at Whitehall, and the mifnamed "Wol-" fey's Hall," at Hampton Court, wherein Shakefpere's company performed before the king in the winters of 1603 and 1604,

are

are chambers for ever affociated with the hiftory of England; and not among their minor affociations is the recollection that in them the King of England liftened to the Poet's plays—faw the Poet himfelf as one of the players—and "be-" ftowed efpecial honour upon Shake-" fpere," in "an amicable letter." The letter was in the poffeffion of Sir William Davenant as reported, and there feems no reafon to queftion the truth of the report. But whether it be true or not, there is no queftion regarding the enactment of the tragedies and comedies before the Court at Whitehall and Hampton. We are thus enabled to interweave the memory of our Poet with two ftructures utterly diffimilar in architectural detail, but each a princely pile, and each clofely connected with the moft ftirring events of hiftory.

Prince Charles, a child of four years
of

of age, may have sported at the King's knee, and witnessed the deed of blood done by the Moor in the same hall through which he was to pass to a darker deed of blood years afterwards. The history of that Palace of Whitehall is familiar to every schoolboy, but not so familiar that of the two halls which have adorned the Palace of Hampton Court. For contrast, for light and shade in historical painting, what four pictures of sunshine and shower could be more dramatic than a vigorous representation of Wolsey's Banqueting Hall, as it must have appeared when he entertained the French Ambassador,—when the Court Revels was held there after the accession of James, and Shakespere performed in the hall which now occupies the same site as Wolsey's, which was most probably designed by him, but not erected until the 22nd Henry VIII., six years after the Cardinal

Cardinal had left the Palace for ever;—and on the oppofite or fhadowed fide of the picture, when Mary inhabited the Court, liftening to the maffes and prayers of her priefts, praying for her fafe deliverance of an heir to the throne of the realm, which was never deftined to be born; or when Cromwell, in his domeftic gloom, paced up and down that Hall, liftening to the mufic of the "box of whiftles," which Puritanic opinion thought too Popifh for the chapel of Magdalen College, but was a fit inftrument, erected in the Minftrel's Gallery at Hampton, to foothe the throbbing breaft of the Lord Protector.

George Cavendifh defcribes Wolfey's entertainment to the Ambaffador of Francis I. Nearly three hundred bedrooms were fitted up to receive his fuite, each provided with a bafin and ewer of filver, wine and beer veffels of filver, bowls, goblets, and filver fconces.

At

At the banquet, bouffets ftretched acrofs the end of the Hall, having fix fhelves one above the other, crowded with gold and filver plate. During the fecond courfe the Lord Cardinal came in, booted and fpurred, and giving all welcome, took a golden bowl filled with hypocras, and drank to the health of his Sovereign Lord and of the King of France. What a contraft to the fpectacle witneffed on the fame fpot in the following century, when the King-killer, quivering with emotion as his child lay dead in an adjoining chamber, wandered in his folitude about that Palace! There Mary likewife had wandered in her folitude! and there, too, Charles had paffed fome of his bittereft days! Strange affociations thefe, with the Hall in which Shakefpere and his company had performed before Charles's father, and perchance in Charles's prefence!

The

The destruction of New Place, and the loss and destruction of every article of personal property that the Poet bequeathed to his family, excepting one book,—Florio's translated edition of Montaigne (1603), with his signature inscribed,—must for ever remain a matter of the deepest regret. We only know of six signatures of Shakespere. All, save one, are appended to legal documents. The autograph in Montaigne is the only scrap of writing by the Poet which associates us with him in his literary life. However valuable his signature may be, a far higher value attaches to his writing in a book that was one of his companions and friends, and possessed a place in his home, than the mere execution of a hard, dry, legal document. A very interesting account of Shakespere's copy of Montaigne was written by Sir Frederick Madden, which states that it was purchased chafed in 1838 for the Britifh Mufeum, from the Rev. Edward Pattefon, of Eaft Sheen, and had belonged to his father, the Rev. Edward Pattefon, of Smethwick, near Birmingham, by whom, previous to the year 1780, the volume ufed to be exhibited as a treafure, on account of its containing the autograph of Shakefpere. In other words, the book and its autograph were fhown with pride, *and not for fale*, prior to Ireland's forgeries, and the vulgar attempts to imitate Shakefpere's fignature by fuch impoftors as Jordan, "*the Poet of Stratford*," fave the mark!

Sir Frederick Madden fays, and fays properly, "the prefent autograph chal- "lenges and defies fufpicion." The book of itfelf is interefting, apart from its connection with Shakefpere; and as it is a treafure which can only be infpected by fpecial leave, it may be well to publifh its title.

THE

THE

ESSAYES,

OR

MORALL, POLITIKE, AND MILLITARIE
DISCOURSES,

OF

LO: MICHAELL DE MONTAIGNE,

KNIGHT,

Of the Noble Order of ST. MICHAELL, *and one of the* GENTLEMEN
IN ORDINARY *of the French King*, HENRY THE THIRD,
his Chamber.

𝕿𝖍𝖊 𝕱𝖎𝖗𝖘𝖙 𝕭𝖔𝖔𝖐𝖊.

(*⁎*⁎*)

First written by him in *French*,
and
Now done into *English*

By

By him that hath inviolably vowed his labours to the
Æternitie of their Honors,
Whofe names he hath feverally infcribed on thefe his
confecrated Altares.

The First Booke.

To the Right Honorable
LUCIE, CO: OF BEDFORD,
and
LADIE ANNE HARRINGTON,
Her Ho. Mother.

The Second Booke.

To the Right Honorable
ELIZABETH, CO: OF RUTLAND,
and
LADY PENELOPE RICHE.

The Third Booke.

To the Right Honorable
LADIE ELIZABETH GREY,
and
LADIE MARIE NEVILL.

JOHN FLORIO.

¶ *Printed at London, by* Val. Sims *and* Edward Blount, *dwelling in Paules Churchyard.* 1603.

That Shakespere was familiar with this tranflation is put beyond all doubt by the fact that, in Act ii., Scene 2, of the *Tempeft*, he quotes from it almoft word for word:—

> "*I' the commonwealth, I would by contraries*
> *Execute all things: for no kind of traffic*
> *Would I admit; no name of magiftrate;*
> *Letters fhould not be known; riches, poverty,*
> *And ufe of fervice, none; contract, fucceffion,*
> *Bourn, bound of land, tilth, vineyard, none;*
> *No ufe of metal, corn, or wine, or oil;*
> *No occupation; all men idle, all;*
> *And women too; but innocent and pure.*"

The paffage thus quoted, in Florio, Book i., Chap. 30, runs as follows:— Speaking of a newly difcovered country, which he calls Antartick France, Montaigne obferves:—" It is a nation—would " I anfwer Plato—that hath *no kind of* " *traffike; no knowledge of letters;* no in-" telligence of numbers; *no name of* " *magiftrate*, nor of politike fuperioritie; " *no ufe of fervice, of riches, or of poverty;* " *no contracts; no fucceffions;* no divi-
"dences;

"dences; *no occupation, but idle;* no "respect of kindred, but common; no "apparell, but naturall; no manuring of "lands; *no use of wine, corne, or "mettle*," &c.

That the volume in question belonged to a library in Shakespere's time, its binding shows, particularly in the Tudor-fashioned *fleur-de-lis* and crown ornamentation with which the leather is stamped.

That the volume belonged to Shakespere himself, the autograph which "challenges and defies suspicion" proves.

Having re-asserted Sir Frederick Madden's words, it would be unfair not to quote the following passage from Mr. Halliwell's "Life of William Shake- "speare," pp. 280-81:—

"It is unnecessary to say that many alleged autographs "of Shakespeare have been exhibited; but forgeries of "them are so numerous, and the continuity of design, "which a fabricator could not produce in a long docu- "ment, is so easy to obtain in a mere signature, that the "only safe course is, to adopt none as genuine on internal
"evidence

"evidence. A signature in a copy of Florio's transla-
"tion of Montaigne, 1609, is open to this objection.
"The verbal evidence as to its existence only extends
"as far back as 1780, after the publication of Stevens'
"fac-simile of the last autograph in the will, of which
"it may be a copy with intentional variations."

Mr. Halliwell's general accuracy makes an error, in what he says of this book, remarkable; and excites the suspicion that, in his scepticism, he may have disdained to give the book that honourable consideration which it really deserves. He says, "translation of Montaigne, 1609." The title above given will show that the date is 1603. The error is hardly worth notice in itself, but well worth it when fallen into by a gentleman to whose painstaking and searching accuracy we are so greatly indebted. It awakens an impression that Florio's Montaigne may be worthy of a closer examination than it has yet received, and may perhaps contain more interesting evidence in favour of its having belonged to Shakespere than

has

has as yet been fhown. For inftance, Sir Frederick Madden, in his defcription of the book, notices the manufcript notes which are found in it, and the quotations and references on the fly-leaves at the beginning and ending of the volume. He ftates that he had at firft hoped thefe notes might have proved to be in the handwriting of Shakefpere, but on examination he concluded they were written at fome period later than Shakefpere's time, though not much later, as the character of the writing proves. There Sir Frederick leaves the matter. But it is well worth while to take the book in hand, and refume its examination at the point where Sir Frederick has dropped it. On the fly-leaf are Italian quotations, references to the claffic poets, and references to fubjects in the book. Thefe prove that the writer was a literary man and a claffical fcholar. Taking up the references, and
turning

turning to the body of the work, we find the margins annotated in several places, and Montaigne's Latin quotations verified or corrected. Sometimes a wrong author's name is given: if so, the annotations correct the press. Sometimes a quotation is given without the name of the author: if so, the annotation throws in " Livy," "Virgil," or some other classical name—such a book, such a line. We are thus put beyond all doubt that the writer was some scholar who had the classical poets, as we say, at his fingers' ends. But here comes the marvel of the matter. Upon the edges of the leaves is printed with pen and ink the name A. HALES.

Hales! Is it possible that the connection of that name with Shakespere entirely escaped the recollection of Sir Frederick Madden, and all other examiners of the book? Did no one remember the Poet's champion at Eton, who Lord

Lord Clarendon declared "was one of the "leaft men in the kingdom, and one of "the greateft fcholars in Europe." Sir Frederick is perfectly correct in ftating that the orthography in the volume, though not Shakefpere's, belongs to a date of the Shakefperian age. When we link together thefe facts—that Mr. Hales, of Eton, was the Poet's enthufiaftic admirer; that he was a profound fcholar, and therefore the very man who would fupply the names of claffic authors to quotations, and correct errors of reference to them, or infcribe on a fly-leaf a parallel paffage from fome Italian poet; that if there was a fale of Shakefpere's goods and chattels at New Place, his books would be precifely the memorials of the man which Mr. Hales would covet and purchafe; that a volume containing his autograph would be a prize eagerly fought and religioufly preferved; that fuch such a work would be read and annotated by Mr. Hales with the intensest pleasure; and that the name "Hales" is actually inscribed upon the edges of the leaves,—it does seem that a strong testimony to the value of the book has been overlooked, and that a most interesting piece of internal evidence as to its historic value has been unappreciated. It is true that it falls short of absolute proof; but the links of the chain couple themselves so naturally, and the probabilities are so strongly in favour of this book having belonged to Mr. Hales, that if such evidence recommends itself to the minds of those who read these pages, Florio's Montaigne must be regarded henceforth with a heightened interest; and just as we regard the book from having passed into the possession of such a man as Mr. Hales, must its preservation by him be an additional testimony—if such were needed—

needed—in favour of the authenticity of the autograph of Shakespere.

Let Hales be "ever-memorable," said Malone, because of his defence of Shakespere. Will he not deserve to be "ever-"memorable," indeed, if it should prove that to his love and reverence we are indebted for the preservation of the only known article of property that belonged to Shakespere?

Thoroughly convinced of the genuineness of the autograph, and strongly impressed with the belief that after Shakespere's death his goods and chattels were sold, and that this book passed into the possession of Mr. Hales, of Eton, Florio's Montaigne is regarded by the author as the solitary "*In memoriam*" of New Place. New Place is swept away; the great house has vanished; the Poet's sword is lost; the plate and jewels are destroyed or sold, or lost likewise; the broad

broad filver-gilt bowl is—melted down perhaps; but one treafure is fpared to us, better than plate or jewels, becaufe it is affociated with the Poet's play of the *Tempeſt*,—becaufe it bears his autograph, —becaufe, being a book, it is a memento moſt kindred to him who has given to the world, fuperior to all other products of the human intellect, the Book of books,—and becaufe, having belonged to his library, we know how he muſt have valued it—

*" Me, poor man! my library
Was dukedom large enough."*

The attention of the reader has been efpecially called to the name of " Charles " Hales," as one of the commiffioners of the inquifition for inquiry regarding the eſtate of Ambrofe, Earl of Warwick. It will be obferved that in Shakefpere's time a Charles Hales is connected with Stratford. Then a John Hales is peculiarly
intereſted

interested in upholding the Poet's fame; and on a book bearing his autograph the name "A. Hales" is found inscribed.

A visit to Heralds' College, and a little of the "Old Mortality" spirit of mural research in Canterbury, Warwick, and Somerset, gives us information of considerable interest, and seems to the author to add value to the folio of Montaigne. The fact is, the Hales family was connected with Snitterfield, and one branch of it was seated there both before and after Shakespere's time. This distinguished stock, which yielded so many servants to the Crown in the high offices of the law, belonged, *ex stirpe*, to Canterbury, and may be traced as located at the Dane John, or Dungeon, of that city, at Hales Place, at Tenterden, and elsewhere. By reference to the appended Pedigree, it will be seen how the junior descents of this house became seated at
Coventry,

PEDIGREE OF HALES.

Nicholas Hales, of Hales Place, Co. Kent.

1. Robert Hales, Kt., Prior of St. John of Jerusalem, and Treasurer of the Sovereign Order in England.

2. Nicholas Hales, Kt., brother and heir of Robert.
   - Thomas Hales, Hales Place, in Haldon, City of Canterbury.
     - John Hales, of Hales Place, son and heir.
       - Henry Hales, of Hales Place and Haldon. = Juliana, fil. et hœres of Richard Cael, of Loden, in Tenterden.
         - John Hales, of Tenterden, in Kent.
         - Thomas Hales. = Elizabeth Cawinton.
           - Sir C. Hales, Kt., Attorney-General to Henry VIII., Master of the Rolls.
             - Daughters, co-heiresses.
               - Honeywood.
               - Edward, of Tenterden. = Margaret, d. of John Honeywood.
               - William. = d. of the Honble. — Brown, of Dodington.
                 - of Royton.
                 - Thomas. = Jane, d. of Thomas Halway.
                   - William.
                   - Martha.
     - Thomas Hales, 2nd son.
       - Jacobus Hales.
         - Johannes Hales, Alderman of Canterbury, 1512.
           - Thomas Hales. =
             - John Hales, ob. s. p.
             - Thomas, of Haldon, Kent. = fil. de Trefroy, of Carmarthen.
               1. (A) John Hales, of the Priory, Coventry, Clerk of the Hanaper. ob. s. p.
                  - Stephen Hales, of Newland, Coventry. = Anne, fil. de R. Morrison, Co. Bucks.
                    - Sir Charles Hales, of Newland, one of His Majesty's Commissioners in the North. Ob. 1615. = Elizabeth, d. of Walter Fisher, of London, and citizen of Coventry.
                    - Thomas.
                    - Anne. = Edward Combe, of "Statton-upon-Havon," Esq. (sic. Harl. MSS. 6060, f. 4.)
                    - Stephen.
                    - Robert.
                      - Sir Stephen Hales, of Newland and of Snitterfield, Knt. of the Bath. Will dated 1668. Bequests to the poor of Snitterfield. = Abigail, d. of W. Myddleton, of Surrey.
                        - Charles Hales, son and heir. Ætat 16, in 1619.
               2. Christopher Hales. = d. of Thomas Lucy, of Charlecote.
                  - (B) John Hales, inherited the Priory, Coventry, from his Uncle John. = d. of Anthony Fonte, Esq., of Co. Leicester.
                    - Bartholomew Hales.
                    - John.
                    - Jane.
                    - Mary.
                  - Prudentia. = John Rul[...], Recorder o[...]
     - Henry Hales, 3rd sno.

Coventry, at Newland near Coventry, and at Snitterfield. John Hales (A) acquired the celebrated Priory of Coventry, which fingularly enough had been granted by patent of Henry VIII., dated 28th July, 37th anno., to John Combes, Efq., and Richard Stansfield, their heirs, &c. From them it paffed to this John Hales, in the 15th of Elizabeth. He died feifed thereof, leaving it to John, his nephew (B), fon of his brother Chriftopher, who, it will be obferved, had married the daughter of Lucy of Charlecote.

If the reader will glance over this Pedigree, it will be obferved that the Halefes, Lucys, and Combes became connected by marriages between their families; and it is of fome intereft to find that fuch a magnificent monaftic eftablifhment as the Priory of Coventry—magnificent even in the wreck that remains of it to the prefent time, converted as it is

to

to be a home for the poor—belonged to the father or grandfather of John à Combe, and after him to the Halefes of Warwickfhire.

The reader will perhaps accufe the author of taking him a heavy ride acrofs heraldic country to arrive at a very fimple fact. But in thefe matters of refearch there is no royal road to knowledge, and it is only by patient fearch that we arrive at a knowledge of facts calculated to throw light on fubjects like the prefent.

The pedigree of Hales, if given in all its branches, would require the infertion of an immenfe map-like fheet in this place, and therefore it is neceffary to exclude fuch branches as are not connected with the hiftory of Shakefpere. As the Halefes wandered away from Kent to Warwickfhire, to Coventry, to Snitterfield, to Newland, fo one of the branches took root in Somerfetfhire, at a place called

PEDIGREE OF A BRANCH OF THE HALES FAMILY.

(HALES *of High Church, Somerset.*)

Hales =

Richard Hales = d. of — Beauchamp, Esq.
of High Church, near Bath, Esq.

John Hales = Joanna,
of High Church, Esq. d. of Thomas Burnham, Esq.

Edward Hales = Ann,
of High Church, Esq. d. of — Grenfield, Esq.

William. David. Susan. Maria.

(C) | (A) |
ANTHONY. JOHN. Anne. Gertrude. Cicelie. Melior.
THE EVER
MEMORABLE JOHN HALES
OF ETON.
Born April 19, 1584.
Obiit May 19, 1656.

(B)
John Hales = Bridget,
of High Church, Esq. d. of Robert Gouldesborough
of Knahill, in the Co. of Wilts, Esq.

Edward. Matthew. Robert. Thomas.
ob. s. p.

Marvyn = Alice,
d. of Richard
Thomas of
Bishop's Nottle, in the
Co. of Wilts, Esq.

John.
Ætat. 10, in 1623.

called High Church. To this branch the "ever-memorable John" belonged. His life is familiar to Eton and Oxford men, and to perfons interefted in Laud, and the Royalift troubles. It is not generally known; and therefore a few words on the fubject may not be inopportune, as John Hales has always appeared to the author to have been the firft fcholar in England who recognifed, as it deferves to be recognifed, the genius and tranfcendent fuperiority of Skakefpere to all the poets of ancient or modern days.

He was, as the Pedigree fhows (A), the fixth fon of John Hales, of High Church (B), and was born in 1584. He matriculated at Corpus Chrifti College, Oxford, April 16, 1597, and took his B.A. July 9, 1603; was elected Fellow of Merton, October 13, 1606; took his M.A. in 1609; and was admitted Fellow of Eton, May 24, 1613. He
accompanied

accompanied Sir Dudley Carlton to the Hague as his chaplain, and was admitted to the Synod of Dort, with reference to which he wrote his "Golden Remains." His connection with the Synod gave a ſtrong Arminian turn to his opinions, and, as he himſelf expreſſed it, he "bid " John Calvin good-night."

In February, 1619, John Hales returned from the Synod, and took up his reſidence in England; but his peculiar theological opinions rendered him obnoxious to Laud, who ſummoned him to a lengthened interview, in 1638, at Lambeth Palace, when, by mutual explanations, Laud and Hales became reconciled, ſo that a very ſhort time afterwards the Archbiſhop, at a public dinner, preſented Hales to a canonry at Windſor, into which he was inſtalled June 27, 1639, though in 1642 he was ejected from the ſame. About the time of
Laud's

Laud's death, 1644, he retired from his rooms in Eton College, and took up his refidence in a private chamber in Eton, where he concealed himfelf for a quarter of a year, in order to preferve the College books and keys, of which he was Burfar. He lived upon bread and beer, and in his concealment was fo near the College, that he ufed to fay, "thofe who fearched "for him might have fmelt him if he "had eaten garlick." He refufed to take the Covenant, and was confequently regarded as a malignant, and ejected from his fellowfhip at Eton. There are many conflicting ftories about his poverty, and the dire neceffity in which he was compelled to fell, for £700, a part of his library to Cornelius Bee, a London bookfeller. This ftatement, however, obtains weight from the confirmation of Dr. Pearfon, who wrote the preface to "Golden Remains."

John

John Hales died May 19, 1656, and was buried in Eton College Chapel-yard, where a monument was erected to his memory by P. Curwen, Esq., and in 1765 an edition of his works was published, edited by Lord Hailes.

The following extracts from his will, taken from the Eton College Regifter, are interesting:—

"I, JOHN HALES, of Eton, &c. &c., do dispose
"of the small remainder of my poor and broken
"estate in manner and form following:—1st. I
"give to my sister, CICELY COMBES, £5.....
"Moreover all my Greek and Latin books I give
"to my most deservedly beloved friend, William
"Salter of Richkings, Esq..... All my English
"books, together with the remainder of all moneys,
"goods, and utensils whatsoever, I give and be-
"queathe to Mrs. Hannah Dickenson of Eton,
"widow, relict of John Dickenson, lately deceased.
"In whose house ... I have for a long time been
"with great care and good respect entertained—
"and her I do by these presents constitute and or-
"dain my sole executrix..... As for my funeral,
"I ordain that at the time of the next Evensong
"after my departure my body be laid in the
"Church-yard

"Church-yard of the Town of Eton, . . . in plain
"and simple manner, without any Sermon, or
"ringing of the Bell, or calling of the people
"together, without any unseasonable commessa-
"tion or compotation, . . . for as in my life I have
"done the Church no service, so I will not that in
"my death the Church do me any honour."

It will be obferved in the above detailed facts, that John Hales had taken his degree at Corpus Chrifti College thirteen years before Shakefpere died, and that he was a Fellow of Eton three years prior to that event. Alfo, that — doubtlefs owing to the family connection with Snitterfield—Cicely Hales, his fifter, had married into the family of Combe ; and laftly, that John Hales's younger brother was named Anthony Hales (C). When we come to put all thefe facts together, there can be little doubt as to the origin of John Hales's peculiarly ftrong intereft in Shakefpere ; and the ink-printed name A. HALES, on the edges of the leaves of the

the copy of Montaigne, gives additional value to that already moſt valuable volume; becauſe we gather from that name, and from the ſcholarly comments and notes in the book, that John Hales, after Shakeſpere's death, had poſſeſſion of this work,—had annotated it with his own erudition,—and that from him the book paſſed to the poſſeſſion of his brother Anthony! It appears to the author that this circumſtantial evidence is as convincing as any ſuch evidence can be, ſhort of a poſitive entry on the fly-leaf to that effect. That the book ſhould have remained in families connected with Warwickſhire, is moſt natural; and that it ſhould belong to a clergyman in the ſame neighbourhood in 1780, is preciſely what we ſhould expect. Let it be remembered that Mr. Patteſon exhibited the book to his friends as bearing the Poet's ſignature for no mercenary purpoſe, and with

with no view of making a sale of it. He valued it as it deserved, and sacredly preserved it. His son was induced to part with it to the British Museum, because it was urged on him that such a book ought to be deposited in the National library.

The reader, and particularly the antiquary, will pardon this lengthened diversion regarding the "ever-memorable " John" and his family; for, believing, as the author does, that the name A. HALES has enticed him into a research which he would otherwise have overlooked, so he believes it has furnished additional evidence in support of Sir Frederick Madden's paper, and—if such were needed—confirmed the authenticity of the autograph in the only remaining book that belonged to the Poet.

Until faith can be driven by overpowering proofs into the wildest infidelity,
let

let us cling to the belief that the autograph is genuine, and that this volume did belong to our Shakefpere. Should that laft plank, which floats us over the gulf of feparation that has gone on widening for more than three hundred years, ever drift away, and leave us utterly cut afunder from the domeftic life of the man, we fhall ftill have, in two of the Palatial Halls of England, monuments that muft be for ever affociated with the genius and glory of the High Prieft of literature.

A mile away from the Hall in which Shakefpere charmed his King and the Court, is the Villa to which one of his chief interpreters, David Garrick, retired, after leaving his profeffion. It is now faft approaching a century fince he too fhuffled off this mortal coil! Half a century after Shakefpere's death, all the tangible affociations connected with him feem to have perifhed, or to have been removed from

from Stratford! Not so at Garrick's Villa, when a whole century is well-nigh complete since his death. His Villa, his garden, his river-side pleasure-grounds, his temple erected to Shakespere, remain as he left them. There is the lawn skirting the Thames, overhung with noble trees, which Garrick showed with delight to Dr. Johnson, and received from the Doctor, as he surveyed the beauty of the scene, the moralising rejoinder, "Ah, David, these are the "things that make Death terrible!"* There is the tunnel under the road, suggested by the Doctor;—"Well, David, "if you cannot get over the road, "try and get under it." There is the drawing-room with the Chinese-patterned

---

* This anecdote was told me by the Rev. Edward Phillips, of Surbiton, to whose family Garrick's Villa now belongs. The story is associated with the place, and is possibly now published for the first time.

terned papering, the palm-tree fashioned fireplaces, the chairs and sofas, exactly as he left them. There is his bedroom, with its presses, its furniture, its bed, and chintz hangings, so long delayed in passing the Customs, that David assured his Majesty's officers Mrs. Garrick was breaking her heart over their delay. Could Garrick return to Hampton and re-visit his home to-morrow, he would find it, its furniture and appointments, as if he had only left it yesterday. The reverential spirit in which this Villa has been preserved, and the furniture of Garrick's drawing-room and bedroom respected, is above all praise. In the lapse of time, through whatever hands the property may pass, let us hope that centuries to come will find these chambers exactly as they are now, at the close of the first century since the great tragedian's death. But how painful is the contrast between

Stratford-upon-Avon. 259

between the confervative action exhibited at Hampton, and the deplorable, nay, wicked, neglect, which prevailed at Stratford!

A volume of fuch intereft and importance as Montaigne's "Effays," publifhed in 1603, is precifely the fort of work which we fhould expect to find on Shakefpere's bookfhelf. Florio's tranflation recommends itfelf *becaufe it is a tranflation*, fince it has been fatisfactorily proved to us that Shakefpere's knowledge was largely, if not entirely, gathered from tranflations of Claffical, French, and Italian authors; and, moreover,—the character of Montaigne's mind being peculiarly calculated to intereft Shakefpere,—had the volume in queftion bearing his autograph not exifted, it might with fome confidence be argued that a tranflation of fuch a famous author, publifhed about 1603, by a near relative of Ben Jonfon's, with whom

whom Shakespere was probably personally familiar, would be precisely the sort of book of which the Poet would possess himself, and in which we should expect to find his autograph. Let a catalogue of all the books published in or about that date be placed before any one familiar with Shakespere's cast of mind, and it may be asserted, without fear of contradiction, that were he about to make a purchase out of the lot, one of the first he would select would be Montaigne.

Here, at the threshold, our curiosity to learn something of the favourite books which the Poet may have had about him is cut short. We know nothing of the sources of his learning beyond such internal evidence as his plays and poems afford. If they carry us over the threshold, they take us no further. They favour us with no glimpse of the sanctum—

tum—of the reading-ftand, the worktable, the inkhorn, or the book-prefs. What early advantages Shakefpere poffeffed—whether from the fchool " i' the " church," or other fources—continue a profound myftery up to this time; though there yet remain quarters for inquiry where fome information might be gathered. The earlieft reliable evidence of Shakefpere's being in London dates in 1589, when he was twenty-five years of age. It is poffible he may have been connected with London for a year or two previoufly, but certainly not longer. Until he was twenty-three or four he refided at Stratford; and this fact fupports the opinion that it was in Stratford the whole groundwork of his knowledge was obtained, as it was in Stratford, in later life, that the greateft achievements of his genius were accomplifhed. Imagination alone can aid us to picture him at

New

New Place when he was comparatively wealthy, able to purchafe property and tythes in Old Stratford, Welcombe, and Bifhopton, and to carry on profitable tranfactions in corn or wool. In his home he had but one child, Judith, who remained unmarried until the year previous to his death! Poor Hamnet, her twin-brother, died the year before they moved into New Place! Mrs. Shakefpere and this daughter were his conftant companions. His other daughter and her hufband, Dr. Hall, lived hard by, and had made a grandfather of him when he was only forty-four years of age. A grandfather! when many Englifhmen, as Johnfon expreffed it, "having frifked "with the dogs," are only beginning to think about marriage, now-a-days!

The glimpfes we catch of him as he paffed along the laft ftage of his life are very few, and fcarcely take us into his home.

1571

THE ANCIENT CHALICE AND PATEN OF BISHOPTON,

From which SHAKESPERE *is said to have received the Holy Communion.*

(It will be observed that the lid of the Chalice, when inverted, forms the Paten, upon the top of which is engraved the date, 1571).

Face p. 262.

home. Bufinefs tranfactions connected with his purchafes at Stratford or in London; the poffeffion of corn; a vifit to London in 1614 to oppofe the enclofure of lands at Stratford,—thefe and a few other facts of a like character are all the information regarding him that has reached us. There is infinitely more fatisfaction in mufing over a couple of lines in Rowe's Life, becaufe their ftatement depends upon Betterton's inquiries, made at Stratford a few years after Shakefpere's death. He fpent his later days " in eafe, retirement, " and the converfation of his friends."

The words may be applied to the laft years both of Shakefpere and of Milton. In retirement and (poor though Milton was) at eafe, and enjoying the converfation of their friends, their countrymen muft love to contemplate England's moft illuftrious fons—the Epic and Dramatic Laureates of the Saxon tongue. Of the
domeftic

domeſtic ſcene at Bunhill Fields we know enough to be enabled to picture it. We even know that Milton enjoyed his evening pipe while joining in the fireſide talk. We know his daily habits; his hours of ſtudy; his writings in London and at Chalfont. It is poſſible that Milton, in that year 1614, when Shakeſpere was in town, may have ſeen him paſs down Bread Street, Cheapſide, to the "Mer- "maid Tavern,"—that patriarch of London Clubs—there to enjoy a ſtoup of liquor and a jeſt with rare Ben Jon- ſon. And yet, while a maſs of the moſt intereſting information exiſts regarding the life of the younger of theſe poets, who were actually contemporaneous, nothing ſurvives to admit us into the home and ſociety of him who Milton calls "our "wonder and aſtoniſhment"—

"*Dear ſon of memory, great heir of fame*,"

There are two circumſtances connected with

with his laſt days at New Place with which we are acquainted. "In perfect "health and memory, God be praiſed," he had his Will drafted 25th January, 1616. February 10th, his daughter Judith married Thomas Quiney. We are led to conclude that the Will was probably drawn up in January with reference to his daughter's marriage; and that ſubſequent to the wedding, Shakeſpere was ſeized with ſome ſudden illneſs, which led to the execution of the Will on the 25th day of March. Theſe few facts, occurring in the firſt three months of the year 1616, conſtitute the entire knowledge we poſſeſs of the cloſing days of Shakeſpere's life. Forty years after his death, the then vicar of Stratford, Mr. Ward, jotted down ſome of the ſtories current in the place regarding the Poet. Among others, he ſtated, " Shakeſpear, Drayton, and Ben Jhonſon
" had

"had a merry meeting, and, itt seems, "drank too hard, for Skakespear died of "a feavour there contracted."

When we remember that Shakespere died in the prime of life, and that he was in perfect health and memory twelve weeks prior to his decease, it seems likely enough that fever was the cause of death. The wedding of Judith would perfectly account for Ben Jonson and Drayton being his companions at Stratford at such a time, though no evidence has as yet been produced to prove Jonson's whereabout at that date. The story of drinking too hard is susceptible of explanation in the same way; and it is easy to be understood how the conviviality of a wedding party at New Place would be converted, on the tongues of gossips, into "hard "drinking at a merry meeting." Village stories and traditions, as it has been already admitted, are worthy of consideration

fideration, but not of truft. They are feldom abfolutely true in themfelves, and yet they almoft always direct the hiftoric inquirer in the right direction to arrive at truth. Traditions are like photographs —diftorting the prominent features of the fubjects they reprefent. Accepting the reverend vicar's ftory as a Stratford tradition, told him in the rough-and-ready phrafeology of the place, and tranflating the meaning of "hard drinking" into the joyous feftivity which would be naturally obferved at fuch a period as the wedding of the Poet's daughter, when friends like Ben Jonfon and Drayton were gathered around the board of their old companion, to drink to the health and happinefs of the bride and bridegroom,— we have a domeftic picture prefented to us of the laft days of Shakefpere, as happy in itfelf as it is probable from its confonance with his character.

Though

Though the picture is the bareft fketch, yet its touches are true to nature; and all, fave one, we know to be true in fact. That one, (the coarfenefs of its colouring toned down), harmonifes well with the reft, and gives completenefs to the outlines. Let fancy fill in the canvas, and the autumn days of the Poet's life be painted in the golden tints of nature's own autumn time, in which funninefs and fadnefs fo myfterioufly blend. Pleafant it is to think that the happinefs of New Place was not fhadowed by any tedious or agonifing ficknefs. There was no lingering difeafe, no protracted pain. "In perfect health "and memory, God be praifed," our Shakefpere lived until his fifty-fecond year. He enjoyed his Merry Chriftmas, and the converfation of his friends. Then came the preparations for the wedding. New Place was all alive. Mrs. Shakefpere's fecond-beft bed, like enough, was aired

aired and made up for the arrival from town of Ben Jonſon. Shakeſpere thought the time befitted that he ſhould make his Will, which was accordingly drafted. The great garden was neatly trimmed, no doubt, and the borders of ſnowdrops and crocuſes fringed the beds about the mulberry tree. The wedding-day arrived. Parſon Rogers, the vicar, appeared in his beſt caſſock, bands, and tippet; and robed in clean white linen ſurplice, leaned against the tomb of John à Combe, book in hand, until the wedding party came. Coaches in Stratford were unknown; but

" Slowly—stately—two by two,"

the train of relatives and friends proceeded from New Place to the church. The merry marriage-bells rang out their welcome, and William Shakeſpere, leading Judith through troops of friends,
preſented

prefented her at the altar to the vicar, and gave the woman to the man.

There were no fignatures of witneffes to the ceremony neceffary, elfe had we feen, perchance, Shakefpere's and Rare Ben's upon the fame page of the Regifter.

The ceremony over, and the vicar unrobed, the whole party left the church. It was the laft time Shakefpere entered it alive, and the laft time he left it! The wedding of his child brought him there that day: about nine weeks afterwards his children attended in the fame place at his funeral! But on that marriage morn none dreamt of, or anticipated, the impending lofs which not New Place only, or Stratford, but England and her literature, were to fuffer. The marriage tables were fpread; the cakes and ale were plentiful; and Parfon Rogers, garnifhing his periods with Latinity, after the fafhion of his day, told how one of old time, in a little

little town of Galilee, had bleſſed with
His preſence that marriage-feaſt at which
the "water ſaw its Lord, and bluſhed!"

> "*Meanwhile the day ſinks faſt, the ſun is ſet,*
> *And in the lighted hall the gueſts are met;*
> *The beautiful looked lovelier in the light*
> *Of love, and admiration, and delight.*"

It was a merry, happy evening in Stratford! No doubt the Haiefes, and the
Quineys, the Hathaways, "my Couſin
"Green," Thomas Combe, and all the
lads and laſſes of the varied Shakeſpere
connection, as far as Warwick, had collected at New Place to celebrate the
wedding,—to "dance and eat plums;"
to be merry with the "round" and
"wooing dance," and to trip it lightly
to the ſtirring notes of "John, come kiſs
"me now!" Subſtituting Ben Jonſon for
"Couſin Capulet," the Poet's own words
beſt ſerve our purpoſe to imagine the
ſcene:—

"*Welcome,*

> "*Welcome, gentlemen! ladies that have their toes*
> *Unplagued with corns will have a bout with you:—*
> *Ah ah, my miſtreſſes! which of you all*
> *Will now deny to dance? . . . .*
> *   I have ſeen the day*
> *That I . . . . could tell*
> *A whiſpering tale in a fair lady's ear,*
> *Such as would pleaſe!—'tis gone, 'tis gone, 'tis gone.*
> *. . . . . Come, muſicians, play.*
> *A hall! a hall! give room, and foot it, girls.*
> *More light, ye knaves! and turn the tables up,*
> *And quench the fire, the room is grown too hot.—*
> *Nay, ſit, nay, ſit, good Couſin Capulet,*
> *For you and I are paſt our dancing days!*"

So, while they went on with the dance, and joy was unconfined, we can imagine theſe *patres conſcripti* of Stratford, gathering together in a knot, and the "natural wit" of Shakeſpere, goaded into point and brilliancy by Ben and Drayton, burſting forth into corruſcations of fancy! Then the reminiſcenſes of London life, of Blackfriars and the Globe, would come up, and the experiences of theſe wits would aſtoniſh and delight their country friends. Shakeſpere could tell many an anecdote of kings and courts, of Whitehall and

and Hampton; and, perhaps, among the jovial pledges of the supper, Ben Jonson might let slip something about Gunpowder Plot. Such a "merry-meeting"—the celebration of his daughter's weddingday—we have sufficient reason for supposing, presents us to Shakespere at New Place, in health and vigour, for the last time. A fever seized him. A few brief days of sickness intervened. Gradually the strength of the hale man succumbed before the invading enemy. Necessity compelled the Will to be signed. Gloom possessed the lately happy, festive, house. At Chapel Street corner, with whispered words and solemn head-shaking, the friends of the dying man told their worst fears. Then there was another gathering! In Holy Cross, most like, the Church's prayers were heard for him who lay a-dying. By his bedside Vicar Rogers would stand, calming the woes

woes of the living, and pointing to the hopes of the dying; while gradually—but painlessly as fever does its work—the last enemy stole in among the group, and the windows of New Place were darkened, and the doors were shut, and the keepers of the house trembled, and the mourners went about the street, because man goeth to his long home! " The " rest is silence!"

As regards the identification of Shakefpere's refidence, there is a popular error. Many writers, and even fome of the lateft, affert that the Sir Hugh Clopton who fucceeded to New Place in 1719, " repaired and beautified it, and built a " modern front to it."

This ftatement is repeated in numerous works down to the prefent day. It is not a mere error; it is more than an error, for it is totally untrue. The evil refulting from it is, that defcribers of New Place, whofe works are efpecially read by vifitors to Stratford, have betrayed the public into a very undeferved amount of regret for the deftruction of the Rev. Francis Gaftrell's houfe, in 1759; that being the houfe to which

which a "modern front" is reprefented to have been added; the original ftructure of Sir Hugh Clopton being encafed within it, juft as the monaftic Zion Houfe is enclofed within that ponderous ducal pile on the banks of the Thames, which looks like a "Union" outfide, and is decorated as an Italian Villa infide. Thoufands of perfons have mourned Mr. Gaftrell's deftructivenefs, caring nothing for the "modern front," but grieving over the antique interior, where Shakefpere was fuppofed to have lived and died.

It is defirable that the public fhould be fet right concerning this miftake, and underftand, that, about the year 1720, one Sir Hugh Clopton utterly demolifhed the fabric which another Sir Hugh Clopton, about the year 1490, had erected. It was not a "modern front," but an entirely new houfe, which was erected about 1720; and it was this ftructure (of the Dutch

NEW PLACE: *as it appeared when rebuilt, circa* 1720.

This is the house in which Garrick was entertained, and which was destroyed by Gastrell.

(AN EXACT COPY FROM THE ORIGINAL DRAWING.)

Face p. 277.

Dutch William or Queen Anne's ſtyle of building) which, devoid of all hiſtorical aſſociation, the ruthleſs Gaſtrell razed to the ground.*

Repreſentations of this houſe are extant. They only need to be examined, and the eye learns inſtantly that a complete rebuilding, and not a "modern "fronting," muſt have occurred in or about 1720.

Upon the ground-floor the hall door occupied the centre, flanked right and left with three windows.

On the firſt-floor a row of ſeven windows were diſplayed, the central one opening into a ſmall balcony. The three centre windows and the doorway, ſlightly projecting, were ſurmounted by a pediment, containing the creſt and motto of the Cloptons, "*Loyavte Mon. Honnevr*," in the tympanum.

The

---

* Appendix K.

The middle of the roof was occupied with a square platform, surrounded by a wooden balustrade, as frequently seen in houses of the period. Rusticated stonework, in long and short blocks, ornamented the corners of the house, and a projecting Classic cornice, with dentile decoration, gave a finish to the roof. On the opposite page this house is represented. In it Mr. Garrick and his friends were entertained at the time of the Jubilee, in 1769.

It was what auctioneers call a substantial family mansion, very square, very flat, very red, and in its flat-topped roof, with wooden balustrades, closely related to the style of structures delighted in by the King of pious and immortal memory.

About Kensington, Chiswick, and Hammersmith, any number of "suitable "residences," built at the same date, may be seen, generally conspicuous as Collegiate

giate fchools, or Claffical and Commercial academies.

However ponderous, raw, and felf-afferting the architecture of that period may be, let it be confeffed that it is infinitely grander, more ftately, and more *real* than that pretentious ftyle now prevalent in London, in which " whatever is, " is not," and a muddy ftucco is falved over the carcafes of houfes to make them look what they are not—fubftantial.

The name of the Rev. Francis Gaftrell was execrated in Stratford. He committed great offences againft the town. This perfon appears to have been the fon of Dr. Gaftrell, Bifhop of Chefter, and to have held the living of Frodfham, in the diocefe of Chefter.

He married Jane, the daughter of Sir Thomas Afton, Bart., whofe family was feated at Afton, in Chefhire. At Stow Houfe, Stow, a fuburb of Lichfield, about

half

half a mile to the east of the Cathedral, lived Elizabeth Aston, sister to Mrs. Gastrell, and, as is usual with spinsters when arrived at a mature age, commonly designated "Mrs. Aston."

Subsequently to the Rev. F. Gastrell's death, his widow lived on Stow Hill, in a house adjoining her sister's.

Letters addressed by Dr. Johnson to this lady are given in Boswell's Life, as also several to Mrs. Aston. With both these ladies Johnson had been intimately acquainted from his earliest years; and the intimacy continued until the day of his death. The following paragraphs from one of his letters will give the reader sufficient evidence of the terms on which Johnson lived with these friends:—

"Bolt Court, Fleet Street,
"*January* 2, 1779.

"Dear Madam,

"Now the New Year is come, of which I wish you "and dear Mrs. Gastrell many and many returns, it is "fit that I give you some account of the past year.

" In

" In the beginning of it I had a difficulty of breathing, and other illnefs, from which, however, I by degrees recovered, and from which I am now tolerably free... But the other day Mr. Prujean called and left word that you, dear madam, are grown better; and I know not when I heard anything that pleafed me fo much. I fhall now long more and more to fee Lichfield, and partake the happinefs of your recovery. Now you begin to mend, you have great encouragement to take care of yourfelf.

"Do not omit anything that can conduce to your health, and when I come I fhall hope to enjoy with you and deareft Mrs. Gaftrell many pleafing hours.

"Do not be angry at my long omiffion to write," &c. &c. &c.

"Madam,
" Your moft humble fervant,
" SAM. JOHNSON."

There is an old man, by name Mr. Thomas Barnes, now living in Bird Street, Lichfield, who has entered his ninety-firft year. He was born at Chorley, near Lichfield, the firft week in February, 1772. He was brought up a wig-maker, and may be faid to have followed his trade up to the prefent time. Mr. Barnes is in the enjoyment of all his faculties, able to garden, and while gardening to recur with the greateft clearnefs of
memory

memory to the events of his early life. He is perhaps the only person living who can say that he remembers Dr. Johnson. Mr. Barnes informed the author that he clearly recollects Mrs. Aston and Mrs. Gastrell living at Stow; and that he remembers seeing the Doctor walking with these ladies in Boar Street, Lichfield, opposite the Town Hall. Mr. Barnes was also well acquainted with Mr. Peter Garrick, brother of the tragedian, whose house was situate in Lichfield, on the site now occupied by the newly-erected Literary Institution and Probate Office.

Mr. Barnes had no personal acquaintance with Doctor Johnson or his female friends, Mrs. Aston and Mrs. Gastrell, for whom, it is beyond question, the Doctor entertained the warmest and most sincere friendliness of feeling.

In glancing round the walls of Lichfield Cathedral, on the north side of the

great

great weſt door in the nave, and above the door of the ſouthern tranſept, there ſtill ſtand tablets to the memory of Mrs. Aſton and Mrs. Gaſtrell. "Still," becauſe it would be well, for the ſake of the architecture, if thoſe unſightly and unharmonious lumps of maſonry had been removed, in the late elaborate reſtorations at Lichfield, to ſome leſs conſpicuous poſitions. Lichfield Cathedral, as it now appears, will be contemplated for generations to come as a monument whereby to recall the Epiſcopate of Dr. Lonſdale. The lover of church architecture will ponder over and revel in the regenerated lovelineſs of that exquiſite gem of art; and in admiration of the ſpirit and munificence with which the clergy and gentry of the dioceſe have gathered round their venerated Dioceſan, in carrying out the glorious work which has been accompliſhed, contraſt it painfully with ſome of
its

its sister edifices, where Cathedral bodies are much richer, and far more able, but apparently much less willing, to encounter the sacrifices necessary for much-needed restorations. To wit—look at Durham, a Golden See! That monarch of all Norman piles is still disfigured with filthy white-wash and yellow-wash. The condition of its nave is a disgrace to any Cathedral chapter; and, as if to prove that ecclesiastical barbarians still survive, those stupendous pillars—the glory of the Palatinate—have very lately been outraged by having glistening lead gas-pipes nailed to their sides, surmounted with fittings and shades of the commonest and most vulgar description!

As it will be necessary to say a few words respecting Mrs. Gastrell with regard to the destruction of the mulberry-tree, it may be the most chivalric if we anticipate her blame by sounding her praise,

praise, and administer the antidote before the bane. The following inscription on her monument in Lichfield Cathedral is a grandiose specimen of testamentary gratitude:—

" J. G. died October 30, 1791, aged 81.

" Sacred to the memory of Jane, daughter of Sir
" Thomas Aston, of Aston, Baronet, and widow of the
" Rev. Francis Gastrell, Clerk, who, to the last moments
" of her life, was constantly employed in acts of secret
" and extensive charity, and on her death bequeathed
" to numerous benevolent institutions a considerable
" portion of her property. This monument was erected
" by her five nephews and three nieces, who partook
" equally and amply of her bounty.

" *Let not thy alms, the holy* JESUS *cried,*
Be seen of men, or dealt with conscious pride;
So shall the LORD, *whose eye pervades the breast,*
For thee unfold the mansions of the blest.

" *O'er her whose life this precept held in view,*
A friend to want, when each false friend withdrew;
May these chaste lines, to genuine worth assign'd,
Pour the full tribute of a grateful mind.

" *Sweet as at noontide's sultry beam, the shower,*
That steals refreshing o'er the wither'd flower,
Her silent aid, by soothing pity giv'n,
Sank through the heart, the dew of gracious heaven,

" *Deeds such as these, pure shade, shall ever bloom,*
Shall live through time and glow beyond the tomb.
Through thee, the orphan owes parental care,
Bends the glad knee, and breathes the frequent prayer;
                                                    Through

Through thee the debtor, from despondence fled,
Clasps his fond babes, and hails his native shed;
Through thee, the slave, unbound his massive chain,
Shouts with new joy, and lives a man again;
Through thee, the savage on a distant shore
His SAVIOUR *hears, and droops with doubt no more.*

" *O thou who lingering here, shalt heave the sigh,*
The warm tear trembling on thy pensive eye,
Go, and the couch of hopeless sorrow tend,
The poor man's guardian, and the widow's friend;
Go, and the path which ASTON *lately trod,*
Shall guide thy footsteps to the throne of GOD."

The Rev. Francis Gastrell appears to have had a great desire to acquire property in, and also about, Stratford. It does not seem that he intended to make New Place a permanent residence, but merely a temporary retreat for pleasure and repose. In his garden stood " Shakespere's " Mulberry-tree," which all visitors to Stratford were curious to see and sit under. Mr. Gastrell's temper was sorely tried by the perpetual invasions of these visitors, and in his spleen he sent forth the fiat to cut it down—" with Gothic bar- " barity," as Boswell remarks. Dr. Johnson

son told him Mr. Gaftrell did fo " to vex " his neighbours." Bofwell adds, " His " lady, I have reafon to believe, *on the* "*fame authority*, participated in the guilt " of what the enthufiafts of our immortal " bard deem almoft a fpecies of facrilege." This facrilege took place in 1756, only three years after Gaftrell became poffeffor of New Place.

The wood of the mulberry-tree was purchafed by Thomas Sharp, of Stratford, watch and clock maker, who manufactured it into boxes, goblets, and a variety of articles for fale. Twelve rings made out of the wood were manufactured for the Jubilee, 1769. A few valuable mementoes ftill remain, highly prized, and carefully treafured.

Among thefe, the Shakefpere chair now in the poffeffion of Mifs Burdett Coutts, and purchafed by her for £300, is the moft valuable. The medallion on the back

back of this chair was carved by William Hogarth.

There is the mulberry cup, which was ufed by Mr. Garrick, and held in his hand when he fang his own fong at Stratford:

" *Behold this fair goblet, 'twas carved from the tree,*
Which, O my fweet Shakefpere, was planted by thee!
As a relic I kifs it, and bow at the fhrine,
What comes from thy hand mufi be ever divine:
All fhall yield to the mulberry-tree.
Bend to thee,
Blefi mulberry:
Matchlefs was he,
Who planted thee,
And thou, like him, immortal be!"
Etc. etc.*

W. O. Hunt, Efq., Town-clerk of Stratford, poffeffes a drawing-room table made

---

* The following receipt for the fale of mulberry-tree wood to Garrick is interefting:—

" *9th July*, 1762.

"Received of David Garrick, Esq., by the hands
" of Lieutenant Eufebius Silvefter, Two Guineas in
" full for four pieces of Mull-berry tree, which, with
" the other pieces of the fame tree, I lately delivered
" to the faid Mr. Silvefter for the ufe of the faid Mr.
" Garrick, I do hereby warrant to be part of the
" Mulberry

made of walnut, the top of which is beautifully inlaid with wood from the mulberry-tree. The device is unufual, being formed by a feries of thin rounds, into which a branch of the tree muft have been fawn. A block of wood occupies the centre of the table, the rounds encircle it, and fucceffive circles continue being defcribed, until they reach the exterior frame of walnut within which they are comprehended. The heart of the tree, and the varying rings of the wood, being feen in every round, a piece of furniture has been manufactured which is artiftic as a fpecimen of geometrical

---

" Mulberry Tree commonly called Shakefpeare's tree:
" and faid to be planted by him; and lately cut down
" in the Rev. Mr. Gaftrell's, late Sir Hugh Clopton's,
" garden, in Stratford-upon-Avon.

"*Witnefs my hand*—GEO. WILLES.

" *Witnefs hereto*—
    WM. HUNT, *Attorney in Stratford.*
    JOHN PAYTON, *Mafter of the White Lion there.*"

trical cabinet-making, and invaluable in its hiftorical affociations. This table belongs to a gentleman who beft deferves to poffefs it, both on account of the unflagging enthufiafm he has exhibited in everything that has reference to Shakefpere (efpecially of late in fecuring New Place to the public); and alfo on account of the urbanity he has fhown vifitors to Stratford, who have had the honour of being introduced to him.

In 1759 what was thought a greater, but was in reality a minor offence, was committed. Being compelled to pay the affeffment for the poor at Stratford, as well as at Lichfield, his fixed refidence, Gaftrell vowed that New Place fhould never be affeffed again, and pulled it down.

This has been regarded as an unpardonable crime. It was not fo in reality, becaufe the houfe had no connection with the Poet, as has been fhown. There can be

Stratford-upon-Avon.

be little doubt that had Homer, Dante, Tasso, and Shakespere all lived in that selfsame house it would have mattered nothing to the Rev. Mr. Gastrell. He would have destroyed it, whatever had been its associations.

Even among clergymen, particularly the perverse and obstinate, passion often dominates veneration.

The Rev. Francis Gastrell's disposition is a study; but it is one which cannot be now pursued. It may be allowable, however, to hint, that inquiry may justify Johnson's communication to Boswell. Mrs. Gastrell possibly did more than " participate in the guilt;" and in the murder done upon the mulberry-tree it may hereafter appear that she was the Lady Macbeth, instigating the reverend Thane to deeds of " Gothic barbarity."

A Diary written in Scotland by Mr. Gastrell has lately been presented (among other

other gifts) to the embryo, "Stratford "Mufuem." Hereafter the public will have accefs to this hitherto private MS. It tells nothing of Stratford; but being a diary, it reveals fomething of the ftyle of thought of the man. A very commonplace and unpoetic ftyle of thought it is, but harmonious with what we fhould conceive fuch a man would be. It may not be gallant to the fair fex, but neverthelefs fomething near the truth, to conjecture that Mr. Gaftrell has been abufed over much: that, as in all great crimes, fo in the mulberry-tree flaughter, "there was "a woman in it," aiding, abetting, and, as Johnfon fays, "participating in the "guilt." Malone, in writing to Dr. Davenport, of Stratford, May, 1788, quotes a letter received from a lady at Lichfield, who afferts that it was Mrs. Gaftrell, and not her hufband, who cut down the mulberry-tree. In the fame
letter

letter, Malone's correspondent gives him a history of Mrs. Gastrell's latest performance at Lichfield. Her house on Stow Hill had been let to a lady at the rental of £100. The lady had been very kind to the poor in the neighbourhood. Mrs. Gastrell having had some disagreement with her tenant, took measures to turn her out, and *determined that the poor should derive no benefit from that house again*, which she resolved should remain empty. Malone's correspondent, in great wrath, says, that Mrs. Gastrell is "little better "than a fiend."

In this report there is a coincidence that cannot escape observation. The same feeling which prompted the destruction of the house at Stratford, in order that it might never again be assessed for the relief of the poor, likewise prompted the closing of the house at Stow Hill, Lichfield, that the poor might derive no
further

further assistance from thence. It is hardly possible to resist the conclusion which the peculiarity of these circumstances suggests; and despite Johnson's friendly regard for Mrs. Gastrell, we must remember that it is from his own lips we hear of that lady's participation in her husband's acts. She was undoubtedly a passionate and imperious woman; and if the whole truth were known, it seems very probable that the instigation to the act, if not the carrying it into execution, both in felling the tree and destroying the house, is attributable rather to Mrs., than to Mr., Gastrell.

It has been discovered that there was a Chancery Suit pending between Mr. Gastrell and the Corporation, strengthening a suspicion that hot blood was roused. The public at this moment knows little of the merits of the Gastrell case, or the amount of provocation under
which

which that irafcible divine fuffered. If all the charges againft him regarding the deftruction of the mulberry tree were proved, and he were found guilty as the real criminal, neverthelefs he cannot be found guilty, as he commonly has been, of deftroying Shakefpere's houfe,—fimply becaufe Shakefpere's houfe did not exift for him to deftroy.

From thefe facts above ground, we now defcend to difcoveries recently made below ground.

During the fpring of 1862, that portion of the garden of New Place fronting the main ftreet, Chapel Street, on the weft, and bounded by Chapel Lane on the fouth, was excavated to the extent of about fixty feet fquare. The workmen, having cleared away the foil soil and *débris* over this large space to the depth of eight or ten feet, came upon a series of foundations. Some very interesting facts have been discovered. The leading and most manifest are, that two sets of foundations exist. The one must be those of the mansion built in the Georgian era, *circa* 1720; the other those of Shakespere's own house—the "Great House" which Sir Hugh built *circa* 1490, and in which both he and the Poet "lived and died." Upon this site there never have been more than the two houses in question. For the sake of distinction, let these houses be designated respectively, the "Great House" and the "Clopton House."

It is easy to distinguish the foundations of the one from the other, because the lines of walls in the Clopton House at certain points meet, and intersect the walls of the Great House (especially in the foundations

foundations abutting on Chapel Lane). Where they so meet and intersect, the Clopton foundations are *built over and across* those of the Great House.

Again: the materials of the Great House are for the most part stone, which such foundations—built nearly 400 years ago—commonly were. The materials of the Clopton House are red brick, and in many places the plaster upon the walls of the offices in the basement is still perfect; and not only perfect, but shows the coloured outline of the staircase, leading from the offices up to the first-floor, as clean and black as if it had been painted yesterday.

Various evidences prove the date of this portion of the foundations.

First. The bricks of which the party-walls are built have that bright red colour, and are set together with that peculiar closeness and sharpness of edge,
which

which particularly characterife the period of William, Anne, and George I.

Secondly. The condition of the plafter and painting fhows that they belong to a houfe which muft have been inhabited at a comparatively recent period.

Thirdly. The evidences of habitation revealed in the Clopton foundations prove that they were portions of Gaftrell's houfe, and verify the ftory of its fudden deftruction. The kitchen fire-place was found quite perfect, and the afh-pit filled with the cinders of the coals that may have cooked Mr. Gaftrell's dinner in Stratford the day before he demolifhed the houfe. A great variety of trifling domeftic evidences of this fort abound, fhowing that thefe " Clopton " foundations are the bafement ftory of a houfe of modern ufe, and that the houfe itfelf muft have been erected during the laft century.

Laft

Stratford-upon-Avon.

Laſt of all, the ground above theſe foundations when dug out proved to be a *débris* of plaſter-of-Paris mouldings, cornices, and decorations belonging to the ſtyle of ornament commonly introduced in the houſes of the reigns of Anne and the firſt Georges. When the walls of the houſe were knocked down, this plaſter work was buried in the ruins; but it is now carefully arranged in an adjoining houſe for inſpection.

There cannot be a doubt about the foundations of the Clopton Houſe (1720) being identified.

From them we turn to the much ſmaller but far more intereſting remains of the Great Houſe.

It is evident that the Great Houſe was not reſtored with a "modern front," becauſe there are two diſtinct ground plans; and the Clopton Houſe foundations (as already ſtated) run aſkew to thoſe of of the Great Houfe, interfecting them at very acute angles. It is alfo evident that in laying the walls of the Clopton Houfe a great portion of the foundations of the Great Houfe were cleared away entirely, and that thofe only were left untouched which there was no neceffity to move. Confequently the foundations of the Great Houfe in which Shake-fpere lived are comparatively fmall in extent.

The following facts are illuftrative:—

Firft. In two feparate places Tudor mullions have been difcovered, built into the Clopton foundations, fhowing that fome of the material of the Great Houfe was cleared out and ufed again in laying the external foundations of the modern one.

Secondly. In that portion of the Clopton foundations where the kitchens and offices ftood, the ground exhibits no traces

CHAPEL LANE

CHAPEL STREET

A

G

C

O

B

H

NASH'S HOUSE

Feet 5 0 5 10 15 20 25 Feet

KEY TO THE PLAN

OF THE

FOUNDATIONS: GREAT HOUSE AND CLOPTON HOUSE.

———o———

A. Ancient Well of the Great Houſe.

B. Well, lately diſcovered, which appears to have belonged to Naſh's Houſe.

C. Kitchen Fire-place.

D. Piece of projecting Ancient Wall, belonging to Shakeſpere's, *i.e.* the Great Houſe; conjectured to be the Foundation of the Entrance Porchway.

E. The External Wall of the Ancient Great Houſe, terminating in N, a Fire-place of the Clopton Houſe.

F. The Site of Naſh's Houſe: with Ancient Foundations.

G. The Crown of the Vaulting depoſited in one of the Offices.

H. The Poſition at which the Ancient Mullions have been built into the Clopton Foundations.

I, K, L, M. Cellar Windows in the Clopton Foundations.

N. Fire-place in one of the Offices of ditto.

O. Ditto.

traces of ancient walls, although it is almoſt certain that the Great Houſe entirely covered this ſite, ſince the frontage to Chapel Street, between Chapel Lane on the north, and Naſh's Houſe (the next plot of land on the ſouth, where a reſidence now ſtands, but which never belonged to New Place), is not more than ſixty feet in length.

Two apparent exceptions preſent themſelves, viz., a piece of ancient wall which, extending under the ſtreet, protrudes inwards into the main wall of the Clopton foundations; and a few feet removed from it, in one of the offices, there are the remains of the crown of a vaulting. Both theſe interlopers, looking ſtrangely out of place, are at firſt ſight a complete puzzle. Why they were ſuffered to abide where they now aſſert themſelves, and are undoubtedly in the way, is the natural conjecture.

The

The portion of wall that projects from the foundations (and outward, under the footpath of Chapel Street) is palpably, both from position and construction, part of the Great House, and may probably be one of the foundations of the porchway or entrance of the Great House, which would necessarily require to be very strong, if above the porch (with its ponderous oak beams, and its elaborately carved arcades) there rose an overhanging chamber, with oriel window commanding the street. This is mere conjecture, which, though it seems probably correct, must be taken for what it appears worth.

The crown of the vaulting obtrusively thrusting itself into one of the Clopton offices would be a marvel and a mystery, supposing it to belong to the Great House; but, with all humility, it may be questioned whether it ever did! May it not, after all, be one (and the only one)

one) mafs of vaulting, which did not break afunder when that reverend Samfon pulled down a domeftic Gaza about the ears of his enemies—the Philiftines of Stratford? May not this conglomerate have quietly dropped from its vaulted eminence to the humble pofition on the floor which it now occupies, and (inftantly covered in with lighter materials) have efcaped being dafhed afunder? This fuppofition, if it be correct, would folve a difficulty of which there has, as yet, been no fatisfactory folution offered.

Affuming it to be true, the remains of Shakefpere's Houfe would be the abovementioned (porch) wall, and the main walls of the Great Houfe adjoining Chapel Lane, which the Clopton walls were built acrofs, and interfected, but which remain in their original folid condition. Thefe main walls are preferved the entire depth of the houfe, commencing

cing from the frontage at the junction of Chapel Street and Chapel Lane, and running eastward along Chapel Lane. Having reached the extreme point to which foundations run in that direction (about forty-five feet in depth), they turn at a right angle northward, and continue about twenty feet, when they encounter a fire-place of the Clopton House, built over and upon them, in which they become lost, and are no farther traceable.

These, then, are the very walls of the very house in which William Shakespere lived and died. They are inconsiderable, it is true, but nevertheless far more extensive than any one could have dared to hope; for when we consider that two houses have occupied this site, and (as is evident) the foundations of the former were in a great measure cleared away in order to lay the foundations of the latter,—moreover, when we recall the
passionate

paffionate vexation which caufed the fudden and total demolition of the latter, it is a matter of no fmall fatisfaction to difcover *at leaſt ſixty feet* of the indifputable and veritable foundations of the Great Houfe that Sir Hugh Clopton erected nearly four hundred years ago, furviving the ravages of time and the work of man's deftructivenefs, exhumed and once more brought to light in the middle of the nineteenth century; fo that all who reverence the name and memory of the greateft genius of the world, may identify, and, for themfelves, examine the walls of the houfe in which our Shakefpere lived and died.

In the midft of thefe foundations there has been fimultaneoufly revealed an object of peculiar intereft. It is "Shakefpere's "Well"—the ancient well of New Place. When the labourers made the difcovery in digging out the foundations, it was
choked

choked with the *débris* of the Gaftrell ruins. The well was cleared out, and its quoining ftones were found to be as perfect as ever. On the 5th of Auguft, 1862, another well, equally as ancient, and, if poffible, in a better ftate of prefervation as to its mafonry, was difcovered in the embankment under Nafh's Houfe, at the extreme northern limit of the New Place plot. Two wells attached to the fame houfe feem ufelefs; and therefore it may be conjectured, that although this latter well is now within the boundaries of New Place, it may, at fome diftant period, have belonged to, and been enclofed in, the adjoining freehold, "Nafh's Houfe," which is now included in the New Place eftate. On the morning after the clearance, Shakefpere's well had filled with feveral feet of the pureft and moft delicious fpring water. From the bountiful fupply of this fpring, every traveller can now

Stratford-upon-Avon.

now slake his thirst, and drink of the same well from which the Poet drank.

In the course of the excavations a few articles have been dug up, of no particular interest or value.

At the bottom of the well, a peculiarly primitive flat-candlestick, with long, straight handle, and very small stand for the candle, was found.

A bone-handled knife, with metal ornaments of an antique character.

A number of tobacco-pipe bowls of the time of Charles II.; the bowls very small, and the clay impressed at the elbow with the name of the manufacturer, "Robt. Legg."

Figured tiles belonging to a pavement; glass; and various pieces of iron-work, much corroded.

These, and a vast amount of small articles of domestic use, have been found among the *debris*, which are all collected
together

together at Nash's House for the antiquary's examination and discussion. Among them there may perchance be some trifling objects as ancient as the time of Shakespere; but it would be almost idle to hope that the riddling of the vast amount of earth which has been displaced will bring to light any objects of real value, or capable of being associated with the Poet's tenancy of New Place.

All the boundaries of Shakefpere's Garden—including the " Great Garden "— have been afcertained, and proved by the title-deeds (nearly 100 in number) of the furrounding properties. The whole of this New Place eftate is now purchafed and fecured to the public, with the exception of one plot occupied by a conventicle-like brick building, entitled "The " Theatre." This ftructure has neither age, appearance, utility, nor affociation to recommend it to the public. The fpot where it ftands was never occupied by any former theatre; the building belongs to the prefent century. As a building it is to the laft degree ugly, and might be miftaken for a village Bethel or Ebenezer!

Ebenezer! It is an obstruction and eyesore in Shakespere's Garden; added to which, to complete its condemnation, it is not a theatre at all! Having been converted into a sort of lecture-hall or public room, it suits the purposes either of a Police Court or County Court in the morning, and of Ethiopian Serenaders, Conjurors, and Travelling Wonders at night!

The building belongs to shareholders, who are willing to sell the property for £1,100. In due time it is to be hoped that this hideous fabric will be purchased and swept away, so that New Place may be restored to its former condition as a garden, and preserved as such for ever.

The name of a theatre in Shakespere's Garden, catches the ear, and suggests that it must be connected with the traditions of the place. It is apparent that this structure has no claim to the antiquary's consideration. There is but
one

one building in Stratford that is in any way affociated with the paft—and that is a barn. A barn is ftill pointed out in which Mrs. Siddons is faid to have performed in her youth. The tradition is probably true, becaufe not only was the company of her father, Roger Kemble, accuftomed to perform in Warwickfhire, but her grandfather, Mr. Ward, was in the habit of acting at Stratford. On the 9th September, 1746, this gentleman gave a benefit performance in the (then) Town Hall, in order to procure funds for repainting the buft of Shakefpere on the monument in the church, and reftoring the original colours. The play enacted was *Othello*, accompanied with a Prologue written for the occafion by the Rev. Jofeph Greene. Through Ward, a diftinguifhed man of the prefent generation was connected with a remote dramatic era: the late Charles Kemble, with

with whose person and performances thousands still among us were familiar, was Ward's grandson; and the grandfather was an actor in the days of Betterton. At one of his benefits in Dublin, the celebrated Peg Woffington made her first appearance, according to the statement in Boaden's "Life of Kemble," though his statement "errs in particu-"larity;" for while it fixes the date as April 25th, 1760, the records of the quiet little church at Teddington tell us that on the 3rd of that month, in that same year, Peg Woffington had left life's stage for ever, and was interred on that day, aged 42. The mistake made by Boaden arose from his confusing the year of Woffington's death with the year of her first appearing for the benefit of Charles Kemble's grandfather. The hall in which Ward produced *Othello*, for the purpose of restoring the monument at
Stratford

Stratford-upon-Avon.

Stratford, no longer exifts; fo that the barn which is affociated with the name of Mrs. Siddons, feems to be the fole remaining building in the town within which the plays of the Poet were reprefented in the days that are gone and the years that are fled.

At the commencement of this work it was contended that as great a veneration is felt for Shakefpere by the prefent generation as by any that preceded it. It muft, at the fame time, be admitted that the age is eminently practical. With a revived and increafingly fpreading tafte for the Beautiful, the men of the Iron age demand that the Beautiful fhall be combined with the Ufeful. Englifhmen are ever ready to give their money in honour of a great name; but they ftipulate that it fhall not be wafted on ufelefs useless architecture or unprofitable objects. It has been the purpose of this work to show what use has been made of the money already provided by the public. New Place in its integrity has been secured. Shakespere's Garden is beyond any risks from future sales. The site of the Great House has been discovered. The few remains of foundations have been brought to light. The garden, as yet in a disturbed state, will presently be cleared and restored to its former use. Once again, and for ever, it will be Shakespere's Garden.

In this, a good work has been accomplished. Much is done; but much remains to do. To complete the work well begun, public aid will be necessary, and for that aid the public must be sought. It might be well if those who were concerned in the various purchases of New Place, and have examined all the titles and records connected with it, were to give

to

Stratford-upon-Avon.

to the world a detailed hiftory of them, accompanied by the fulleft plans and illuftrations of the property as it exifted when put into truft in 1861. Hereafter fuch a work, which this fmall volume makes no prefumptuous pretence of undertaking, would be of the higheft value. There are very few men among us competent to perform it; but among the few, Mr. Halliwell has had rare advantages in his connection with the purchafes of New Place, which no one elfe has enjoyed. To him the public feem to have a right to look for that fair and faithful hiftory—that compilation of the facts regarding New Place, which have hitherto been obfcure or unknown, but muft now be beft known to him.

The object with which thefe pages have been written, will be fully accomplifhed if they fucceed in attracting public notice to the good work fo far done, and in ftimulating the aid which is neceſſary to complete the full redemption of the Poet's property. New Place muſt for ever be aſſociated with the memory of Shakeſpere; and the mere ſight of foundation walls belonging to the houſe in which he lived and died, cannot fail to excite the deepeſt intereſt in the minds of all who are attracted to the ſpot by hearing of the recent diſcoveries. But intereſt having been excited, and curioſity having been gratified, a practical purpoſe will be required, ſooner or later, to ſupport the ſentiment, under the influence of which, Shakeſpere's countrymen have purchaſed his garden. We are often aſſured that "opportunity is everything." If not everything, it is unqueſtionably a great thing; and with regard to the ſubject under conſideration, opportunity has reſolved to do her beſt in lending it a helping hand.

The

Stratford-upon-Avon.

The swiftly approaching year 1864 will be the Tercentenary Jubilee of the Poet's Birth. Nearly a century ago (in 1769), the celebration of his nativity was held in Stratford under the direction of David Garrick. A sillier or more useless exhibition was never witnessed. Despite the excitement which it created at the moment in Stratford, there seem to have been some of the inhabitants who spoke of it in contemptuous language, for the "Garrick Correspondence" reveals a passage of letters between the Rev. Mr. Jago,* of Snitterfield, and George Garrick, the brother of the tragedian, showing that the latter had resented some uncomplimentary animadversions of Mr. Jago's upon Garrick and the Jubilee. The brother's resentment was a necessary result, for never was there a more devoted brother

---

* Appendix. L.

brother than was George Garrick to David. A charming illuſtration of this is afforded us in the "tender pleaſantry" of Charles Banniſter at the time of Garrick's demiſe. Whenever George was abſent from Drury Lane for any length of time, on returning, his invariable queſtion to the hall-porter was, "Has my brother wanted " me?" It eventuated that the brothers died within a few days of one another. David Garrick expired at his houſe on the Terrace, Adelphi, early on Wedneſday morning, January 20th, 1779, and was buried in Poet's Corner on the 1ſt of February. On the 3rd of February George Garrick expired. When the report reached Drury Lane, Banniſter obſerved, "His brother wanted him!"

But the admiration and affection of George for David could not draw the ſting of the Rev. Mr. Jago's cutting obſervations. Their ſting lay in their truth

Stratford-upon-Avon. 319

truth. Garrick in one of his letters wrote, "When I was busied about that "foolish hobby-horse of mine, the Ju-"bilee!" His language is as correct a description of it as could be given, though the wet weather kindly interfered to prevent the greatest absurdity of the programme — the " pageant procession " of Shakespere's principal characters." Owing to the tremendous downpour of rain, that pageant was never perpetrated at the Jubilee, albeit, there is in the Town Hall of Stratford, a fire-screen which gives an amazing pictorial illustration of the procession; and there is also a tradition that Mrs. Siddons personated Venus in the Jubilee procession. The screen in question—although it represents a display that never took place,—is well worthy of contemplation. Painted by some village artist, it is as grotesque and amusing a production as any one with a keen sense of
the

the ludicrous, would wish to contemplate. Distant be the day when the Corporation of Stratford remove from their Hall, this humorous representation of an historical event that never took place!

With reference to Mrs. Siddons appearing as Venus in the procession of the Jubilee, it is true that she did personate that part, but not at Stratford. Owing to the procession being washed out of the programme, it was dramatised the following October (1769), at Drury Lane, by Garrick, who introduced into it the songs and the odes that had been given in the Stratford Amphitheatre. We read of it, " Such was the magnificence of the " scenery, and the effect given through- " out the piece, that it was so far esta- " blished in public favour as to cause its " being repeated during the season for " upwards of 100 nights."

It was not even upon this occasion that

that Mrs. Siddons exhibited as Venus, nor, until 1775,—the feafon before Garrick's final retirement, and that of her firft appearance at Drury Lane. Garrick revived the *fpectacle* of the Jubilee Proceffion during the feafon, and the Lady Ann who had trembled in terror before his glance of reproach in the great fcene of Glofter's wooing, was caft to perfonify Venus. Mrs. Siddons, in her Autograph Recollections, alludes to the Jubilee performance:—" He (Garrick) would some-
" times hand me from my own feat in
" the green-room to place me next to his
" own. He alfo felected me to perfonate
" Venus at the revival of the Jubilee.
" This gained me the malicious appella-
" tion of ' Garrick's Venus,' and the ladies
" who fo kindly beftowed it on me, rufhed
" before me in the laft fcene, fo that if he
" (Mr. Garrick) had not brought us for-
" ward with him, with his own hands,
" my

"my little Cupid, (the subsequent auto-
"biographer Thomas Dibdin), and my-
"self, whose appointed situations were in
"the very front of the stage, might have
"as well been in the Island of Paphos.
"Mr. Garrick would also flatter me by
"sending me into one of the boxes when
"he acted any of his great characters."

Such are the facts which connect the name of Mrs. Siddons with the Jubilee Procession, there being no connection at all with the celebration at Stratford, at which, nevertheless, she might have been present; for two years previously (February 12, 1767), Miss Kemble (aged twelve), and her brother, John Philip (aged ten),* had appeared in the parts of the Princess Elizabeth and the Duke of York,

---

* John Philip Kemble was born at Prescot, in Lancashire, February, 1757. The author was, some years since, curate of Prescot, and a frequent visitor of the humble folks who now inhabit the house in which Kemble first

Stratford-upon-Avon.

York, in the theatre at Worceſter, in Havard's tragedy of *Charles the Firſt*, which, though unknown to the modern ſtage, was at one time highly popular, and ſo affecting, that when the part of Charles was performed at Hull by Cummings, the early rival of Kemble, his imperſonation of the miſeries of the King ſo overwhelmed Miſs Terrot, the daughter of a garriſon officer, that her emotions cauſed her inſtantaneous death.

The Stratford Jubilee was celebrated for three days: Wedneſday, Thurſday, and Friday, the 6th, 7th, and 8th of

---

firſt ſaw light. Like many houſes in the neighbourhood, it is built of the prevailing red ſandſtone, and is whitewaſhed. It has ſolidity enough to laſt for centuries to come. In former years, when Preſcot was the firſt town out of Liverpool on the coaching road, thouſands of travellers would paſs by the door of John Kemble's birthplace. It ſtands in the "Lower Road," going from the market-place of Preſcot to the neighbouring railway ſtation of Rainhill; and the good man of the houſe uſed to take pride in ſhowing the bedroom " i' which th' great actor cum i'th' wuld, welly nigh gang a 'undred yeear."

of September, 1769. The town was thronged with visitors from London and the surrounding counties. There were present, among others—

>The Duke of Manchester.
>Duke of Dorset.

The Earl of Northampton,
Earl of Hertford,
Earl of Plymouth,
Earl of Carlisle,
Earl of Denbigh,
Earl of Shrewsbury,
} And their Countesses.

>Lord Beauchamp,
>Lord Grosvenor,
>Lord Windsor,
>Lord Catherlough,
>Lord and Lady Spencer,
>Lord and Lady Archer,
>Lord and Lady Craven;

and a large number of Baronets, Members of Parliament, and County gentlemen. Connected with the drama there were—

>David Garrick, and his brother George,
>Mr. Foote,
>Mr. Colman,
>Mr. Macklin,
>Mr. and Mrs. Yates,
>Mr. Ross (Edinbro),
>Mr. Lee (Bath),

and about one hundred and seventy actors and

and actresses of minor repute from the London theatres.

Among other notabilities present was James Boswell. Dr. Johnson was staying with the Thrales, at Brighton, and could not be induced to honour the Jubilee with his presence. Boswell says, " I was very sorry that I had not his " company with me at the Jubilee in " honour of Shakespeare, at Stratford- " upon-Avon, the great Poet's native " town. Johnson's connection both with " Shakespeare and Garrick founded a " double claim to his presence, and it " would have been highly gratifying to " Mr. Garrick. Upon this occasion I " particularly lamented that he had not " that warmth of friendship for his " brilliant pupil which we may sup- " pose would have had a benignant " effect on both. When almost every " man of eminence in the literary
" world

"world was happy to partake in this "festival of Genius, the absence of "Johnson could not but be wondered at "and regretted."

Perhaps the verdict of posterity may be the reverse of Boswell's. The "Great "Cham" was not partial to buffoonery, and it is probable that he kept away from Stratford because he would not encourage his "brilliant pupil" astride of his "foolish hobby horse."* Johnson had no

---

* A number of letters regarding the Jubilee of 1769, addressed by Garrick to Mr. Hunt, of Stratford (grandfather of the present Town Clerk), are in existence. In one of them Garrick says:—"I heard yester- "day, to my surprise, that the country people did not "seem to relish our Jubilee, that they looked upon it to "be Popish, and that we should raise ye d———l, and "would not. I suppose this may be a joke, but after "all my trouble, pains, labor, and expense for their "service and the honour of yr county, I shall think it "very hard if I am not to be received kindly by them; "however, I shall not be the first martyr for my zeal.
"I am, dear Sir,
"Always in a hurry, but yours sincerely,
"D. GARRICK."

"Pray tell me sincerely what common people say."

Stratford-upon-Avon. 327

no taste for masquerading, which Boswell had. The occasion was propitious. During the day he appeared in the streets of Stratford with the words "Corsica Boswell" displayed in large letters round his hat; and at the evening entertainment he exhibited himself as a Corsican Chief, with "*Viva la Libertà*" inscribed on the front of his cap! Johnson's presence at such fooling, would have been *much to be regretted.*

The only portions of the Jubilee which deserve record, were the performance, in Stratford Church, of Dr. Arne's Oratorio of *Judith*, under the direction of Arne himself, for which he received a payment of £60 from Garrick; and the Oration pronounced by Garrick, in the Amphitheatre. The Odes, which were partly spoken by him, and partly sung, contain nothing to recommend them to our perusal; but one passage from the
"Oration

"Oration in honour of Shakefpere, "written and fpoken by Mr. Garrick," may fitly be reproduced. Alluding to the "ufes" and opportunities of life, at the clofe of his oration, Garrick faid,—

"In thefe fields, where we are pleafed "with the notion of doing him honour, "he is mouldering into duft.

'Deaf the prais'd ear, and mute the tuneful tongue.'

"How awful is the thought! Let me "paufe. If I fpeak, it muft be in my "own character and in yours. We are "men; and we know that the hour "approaches with filent but irrefiftible "rapidity, when *we* alfo fhall be duft. "We are now in health and at eafe; but "the hour approaches when we fhall be "fenfible only to ficknefs and to pain,— "when we fhall perceive the world gra- "dually to fade from our fight, and clofe "our eyes in perpetual darknefs."

Ten

Stratford-upon-Avon.

Ten years subsequently the world had faded from Garrick's sight. Time's course is so rapid, that another centenary Jubilee is close at hand. What men of eminence in the literary world, what nobles or princes of the land, will collect at Stratford—and in what manner the Jubilee is to be conducted—must shortly be considered. It may, however, be suggested to those interested in the restoration of New Place, and to those who will arrange the programme of the Jubilee, that they should remember Garrick's solemn peroration on the "uses" of life, and, especially in this practical age, determine upon soliciting public sympathy and support in April, 1864, for practical purposes, and not for a frivolous pageant to the memory of a great man. The best honour which can be paid to his memory will be the promotion of objects useful to the body of men in connection with whom

whom Shakespere made his name and fame.

That the Tercentenary of his birth should be celebrated at his birthplace is a propriety which every one will recognise; but what *must* be there, may also be elsewhere. There is no reason why the people of the Metropolis should not commemorate the occasion, as well as the select few whose time and means will allow them to congregate at Stratford. Such a double celebration seems almost a certainty. But, whatever be the form of festival held, whether in London or in Stratford, the age we live in, warns all sensible men against the repetition of any such mumming as took place under Garrick's programme of 1769. Foote, who was present, has given us his definition of that occasion:—" A Jubilee is a public
" invitation, circulated by puffing, to go
" post without horses, to a borough
                                    " without

Stratford-upon-Avon. 331

"without representatives, governed by a mayor and aldermen who are no magistrates, to celebrate a great poet, whose own works have made him immortal, by an ode without poetry, music without melody, dinners without victuals, and lodgings without beds; a masquerade, where half the people are bare-faced; a horse-race up to the knees in water; fireworks extinguished as soon as they were lighted; and a gingerbread amphitheatre, which, like a house of cards, tumbled to pieces as soon as it was finished." Foote's caustic humour, if not true in its description of the Jubilee, is perfectly true in outline; the grotesque colouring of the picture is its only untruth.

It is devoutly to be wished, that the follies of 1769, may be a warning to the people of 1864. To begin and end with a show, and to accomplish no permanent good,

good, is not confonant with the tafte of the prefent day. Whether at Stratford or in London, or at both places, the Tercentenary celebrations muft feek the public fympathy on behalf of fome public good. If there were but the one celebration at Stratford, it might be well to devote all the funds collected, to the completion of the propofed purchafes, the laying-out of New Place Gardens, and the erection of fome monumental ftructure, commemorative of the purchafe and of the 300th celebration of the Poet's Birth, but, while beautiful as a piece of architecture, at the fame time a ftructure that fhould be practically ufeful for literary purpofes, and a benefit to Stratford and the nation. In the Metropolis, the refults of a Jubilee celebration, might probably be devoted to fome other object. It appears natural, that the object fhould be Metropolitan; and if fuggeftions were wanted,

numberlefs

numberless schemes, without doubt, would quickly be proposed. But it should never be forgotten that the Jubilee is in honour of Shakespere, and that those have the best claim to enjoy the benefits of the public largess, who, in this day and generation, follow the calling of the man, to whose honoured memory, the commemoration is dedicated.

True it is, there are many who profess a conscientious disapproval of the drama, and who, neither directly nor indirectly, would encourage the "poor player." It may be a subject of regret—but, nevertheless, it is a fact which cannot be denied—that some persons affect to condemn the works of Shakespere himself. With this undoubted fact in mind, it will be desirable, having due respect to tender consciences and hopeless prejudices, to present some object for public sympathy at the Jubilee, which may, if possible, disarm all cavil and objection.

If

If the depreciators of Shakefpere, and the difapprovers of the profeffion to which he belonged, be taken on their own ground—and, for the fake of argument it be momentarily granted that the Puritanical view of the drama is its righteous and proper eftimate; in the fame proportion that its influence is afferted to be evil and deftructive, muft the fympathies and folicitude of fuch perfons, if fincere in their belief, be aroufed on behalf of one helplefs clafs connected with Shakefpere's profeffion. Whatever the player may be, the player's child muft be an object of concern to all who are interefted in the education of the young;—but he muft be doubly fo to thofe, whofe duty it is, in the fincerity of their principles, to attempt the refcue of that child, from influences which they believe deftructive of its foul's welfare!

It

It is to be hoped that the subject of education would present a common ground, whereon diversities of opinions might meet to accomplish, a truly Christian and beneficial object.

In the abundant philanthropy of the present age, schools and institutions have sprung up on every side, wherein the greater the degradation of the young, the greater the sympathy of the professed religious world! The fallen, the friendless, the erring, and the outcast, have been the recipients of Christian compassion and solicitude. Every right-feeling person must pray that God's blessing may protect and prosper our Ragged Schools, our Reformatories, our Penitentiaries, and that they may, in their prosperity, reflect blessings on the heads of all earnest men and women, who, in their support, have practically evinced the first of Christian virtues. But there are spheres

spheres in life, removed alike from absolute want, and association with crime; where sympathy is not less needed, and where respectable poverty — that owes no man anything—shrinks from seeking aid, and values self-dependence with as honourable a love, as the wealthiest and noblest of the land!

Among Shakespere's professional descendants, there are many such, who, owing to the smallness of their salaries, are hindered from procuring for their progeny that sound teaching which every English child should enjoy; and who, constrained by need, are compelled to introduce their offspring in their early years to subordinate situations in the theatres, at a time when the child's moral and physical constitution require, the one bringing up in the way it should go, the other, the vigour derived from regular habits, early rising, early rest, and unbroken repose.

repose. It is unnecessary to point out that the opposite of all this, is the inevitable result of engaging a child in the arduous business of a theatre. The intellect is left untrained, the strength of the body is sapped and undermined, and it is to be feared that in a calling peculiarly open to temptation, moral deterioration may frequently accompany physical exhaustion.

In that Royal College which has been honoured with the patronage of, and has been watched over with interest by, the highest personages in the realm, the design of the promoters is understood to be, not only the provision of homes for decayed actors and actresses, but also the completion of a Dramatic College in the fuller sense of the phrase, wherein childhood and old age may be associated—wherein Spring and Winter may flourish together, and both put forth their seasonable

able flowers. Some of the nobleſt of Old England's charities exhibit this touching union; and never has the ſatiriſt of this age more tenderly moved the hearts of his readers, than in that paſſage of the Newcomes, where the aged brother of the Charter Houſe, liſtens to the chapel-bell calling the ſchoolboys to their prayers, and replies to his own ſolemn ſummons, "*Adſum!*" The Charter Houſe is one of many ſimilar foundations ſcattered about the land. It was a happy thought on the part of thoſe who were moſt earneſt in inſtituting the Dramatic College, to deſire that, within the boundaries of the ſame inſtitution, a ſchool for the player's child ſhould be erected hard by the homes of thoſe who had fallen into the ſere and yellow leaf. The homes are completed, but this good work has not yet been begun!

Is there not, in ſuch an undertaking, a beneficial

beneficial and charitable object, to which the profits of a Metropolitan Tercentenary celebration of Shakefpere's nativity might be dedicated? The education of the children of actors can be objected to by none, and is a righteous and goodly aim, that may properly be approved by all!

It would be a great work accomplifhed—a work of genuine and practical honour to the memory of the Poet, if on a feftival, which can only be celebrated by every third generation, a fufficient fund were raifed for building and endowing with a few " Shakefpere Scholarfhips," a Dramatic College School, wherein the children of the hard-worked and humbly-falaried artifts could be provided with found and liberal education, fitting them, when adults, to take their choice of other callings in life than thofe of their parents, if fo difpofed; but, under any circumftances stances, preserving them in their childhood, from the turmoil, fatigue, premature constitutional decline, and inevitable precocity, of baby actors, and Thespian phenomena.

By the erection of such a school, Shakespere's Jubilee, in 1864, would be made a genuine and abiding Jubilee in the families of hundreds of our countrymen, who are painstaking, striving, and respectable men, — who would bless, with grateful hearts, the friends that sympathise with them in their narrow circumstances,—friends that abhor the assumption of patronage, and cordially embrace a rare opportunity of showing concern and care for the player's children, on the festival which commemorates that red-letter day in England's calendar, when, three hundred years ago, sweet Shakespere was himself a child!

APPENDIX.

****

A—page 16.

The Family of Bott.

Though confiderable information has been difcovered in the preparation of this work regarding the Botts, as given at pp. 75 to 85, neverthelefs, I have not thought it worth while to purfue my inquiries far into their hiftory, as I fhould had there been anything of intereft as regards Shakefpere likely to be arrived at by the refearch.

It will be obferved that I have fpoken in ftrong language regarding W. Bott; and, at p. 86, have called him a "grafping lawyer." From the evidence which has come into my poffeffion in refearches regarding the fales of New Place, I find that Bott muft have been a thoroughly unprincipled, pettifogging attorney, doing all the dirty work of Stratford and its neighbourhood. His character oozes out through the medium of the following proceedings taken in the Star Chamber (*temp.* Elizabeth); and however meagre the details may be, ftill new light is difcernible regarding fome members of his family and his pofition with reference to W. Underhill.

By the Bill of Complaint we are informed that John Harper, of Henley-on-Arderne, co. Warwick, who was poffeffed of certain lands and tenements in Henley, Ownall, Wotton, and Whitley, in the county aforefaid, was in danger of being taken in execution under a diftrefs at the fuit of Sir Edward Afton, Knight. Under which circumftances, being himfelf a plain and
fimple-

simple-minded man, he was induced to seek the assistance of W. Bott, of Stratford, a man of about fifty years of age, and reputed of some experience and ability, to advise him properly.

Bott had two sons and three daughters, and finding his client possessed of some substance, although under age, made up a match between him and his daughter Isabel; and further, on the 10th of April, 1563, devised a deed of feoffment, whereby Harper should assure to him and others, in fee simple, all his lands to certain uses, unknown to the petitioner, but as far as he conceives, to the use of petitioner and wife, and their heirs, &c., with remainder to one of Bott's sons, promising to extricate him from his difficulties, alleging it was for the better advancement of his wife; and that the said deed was only a conveyance of his goods, and "*that because the goods remained in the house, he must make livery of them by the ring of the door.*" The unsuspecting youth fell into the snare, being easily led to do whatever his father-in-law instructed him, who, not content with this, if we may believe the allegations of the petitioner, forged, erased, and altered other deeds concerning the said conveyance; indeed, in the preamble of the bill, which we must bear in mind was framed probably some six or seven years after (Mrs. Harper being dead in the interim, without children), he denounces him as "*a man clearly void of all honesty, fidelity, or fear of God, and openly detected of divers great and notorious crimes, as, namely, felony, adultery, whoredom, falsehood, and forging, a procurer of the disinherison of divers gentlemen your Majesty's subjects, a common barretour, and stirrer of sedition amongst your Majesty's poor subjects.*"

This nefarious proceeding, executed without the consent or privity of petitioner, places him in the position that he cannot lease his lands, &c., without Bott's consent, and that, in point of fact, he is only tenant thereto for life. Having thus wrested petitioner's poffeffions, he withholds too the evidences and muniments of the fame—the contents, and even the number of which are utterly unknown to petitioner. He prays, therefore, a writ of fubpena for W. Bott perfonally to appear and anfwer thefe charges. Thus far the complainant's ftatement.

Bott denies the facts alleged as flanders emanating from complainant and his adherents, and declares that if the premifes were true, it were determinable at common law, and not in the court of Star Chamber, ftating that about fix years ago, complainant being a minor, did marry his daughter Ifabel, at which time he promifed on arriving at twenty-one he would make her a jointure; but inftead thereof, becoming improvident, he mortgaged his lands, and fell into difficulties. Thereupon, coming to his father-in-law in tears, he befought his affiftance, which he readily promifed on thefe conditions, viz., that he fhould affure his eftate, or rather the portion left unfquandered, to himfelf and wife, or the longeft liver of them, then to their iffue, failing which, to the various fons and daughters of the faid Bott in fucceffion, for which defendant undertook to fatisfy Sir Edward Afton and divers other creditors. The catalogue of crimes hurled at his reputation he meets by a countercharge, and declares it to be by the "*falfe and malicious procurement of one William Under-* "*hill and Rowland Whelar, which that the faid defen-* "*dant is ready to aver and prove that the faid Underhill* "*is a ftirrer of fedition, and of a very evil confcience,* "*and fo meet to join with the faid Whelar, a very common* "*barretour and a vagabond.*" Further, he denies the truth of the ftatement about his own procurement of the marriage, for the complainant was married three or four years before the affair of Sir Edward Afton. All the other charges he denies *in toto feriatim.*

The replication of Harper denies the ftatement about the jointure, and that whatever mortgage he made, which would be but trifling, was at Bott's inftigation. The debts, too, as paid by defendant, were of

no

no magnitude; fome eight pounds would cover the whole, including that of Sir Edward Afton, in difcharge of which defendant yet detaineth £9, which petitioner recovered againft Sir Edward, and detains moreover a fum of 40 marks which he promifed to give with his daughter as her dowry, &c.

So far from W. Underhill being meet to be matched with any vagabond, he is, on the contrary, "*a gentle-man of a worfhipful calling in his country, and very well known to all honeft men to be of good eftimation, and of very good name, report, and credit, a maintainer of juftice, and a repreffer of evil doers.*" That Sir Edward Afton's fuit againft petitioner was commenced long before his marriage, is alfo untruly alleged.

The rejoinder by Bott denies generally the truth of the ftatements in the foregoing replication, and fays further that he never did promife complainant any bigger fum than £20, which he did pay before they went to the church to be married, and avers that complainant is maintained and fupported in his flanders by the faid W. Underhill and his companion, Rowland Whelar, as named in the anfwer.

By taking the year 1563 as the date of the marriage, or thereabouts, and adding fix years, the time noted by Bott in his anfwer, the probable date of thefe proceedings would be about 1569.

It will be feen at p. 77, that there was a near relationfhip at one period between the Botts and the Cloptons. In the Domeftic Correfpondence, Eliz., vol. cxxxvii., art. 68, anno. 1580, among the Gentlemen and Freeholders in the Countie of Warwick appears,

"Hundred of Hemlingford,
"George Bott."

In another fimilar work appears,
"Solyhull,
"George Boote."

(Intended for Bott, as there was a family fo named at Solyhull at that date.)

From

Appendix. 345

From various traces of the name, cropping-up in this way, I have fatisfied myfelf that an extenfive family of the Botts was fcattered about Warwickfhire in Shakefpere's time; and if it were worth while, a very flight inquiry in the parifh regifters in the neighbourhood of Stratford would probably fupply abundant evidence concerning them. There was a moment when I entertained the fufpicion that the Botts had been mixed up with fome foul play perpetrated in the Clopton family, in the time of William and Anne Clopton.

On perufing the following documents, any reader would naturally fuppofe, as I at firft did, that a William Clopton, and Anne his wife, living about the years 1580 to 1589, would be the William and Anne marked "C" upon the Pedigree, more efpecially as the circumftance of this William Clopton dying without an heir, gives countenance to the allegations in the following Bill of Complaint. I had not then compiled the Clopton Pedigree, and confequently was not aware that William Clopton (C) lived until 1592, and that Kentwell, in Suffolk, was no part of the property of that branch of the Clopton family feated at Clopton, Warwickfhire. This proves the neceffity for an intimate acquaintance with family pedigrees when we deal with public records, otherwife a confounding of perfons may eafily arife, fuch as in this inftance would be moft natural, where we find documents relating to perfons of particular names at a fixed date, and then difcover that perfons of the fame names—*man and wife*—and at the fame date, lived in another county.

Bill of Complaint of Anne Clopton, &c.*

"Showing that her late hufband, William Clopton,
" Efq.

---

* Proceedings in Chancery, *temp.* Eliz., C. c. 13, No. 3. Date inscribed on the top, 12 May, 1589. Counts of three documents only, the answer of the defendants not appearing to be extant.

"Esq., of Kentwell, in county of Suffolk, leased sundry
"manors and lands to William Clopton of Groughton,
"and another, to pay £40 per annum for the same,
"&c. &c. Thomas Clopton (a brother of the half
"blood to the said William, complainant's late husband)
"used subtle means to obtain the lands from the right
"heirs, persuading the said William Clopton who was
"enfeebled by long sickness, to disinherit his next heirs,
"and to convey his whole estate to the said Thomas
"Clopton, inducing him to make his will by the which
"he left only one legacy of very small amount to one
"of his servants, and nothing to his wife or his sisters,
"or sisters' children, &c. &c. Prays a writ of subpœna,
"&c. &c., as Thomas Clopton, William Clopton of
"Groughton, and John Bowsell, the other defendant,
"have procured the property to be conveyed to them-
"selves, and have made themselves masters of all."

Replication of Anne Clopton to the Answer of William Clopton and John Bowsell:

"States that John Bowsell, defendant, was servant
"to William Clopton, complainant's late husband, and
"that during his long continued illness it was insinuated
"by defendants to William Clopton, that Anne his
"wife, and one Thomas Smith, a nephew of William
"Clopton, employed poison, whereupon she desired that
"she might go away from him for some little time,
"until he were recovered and better persuaded con-
"cerning such slander; to which her husband replied
"that Thomas Clopton was a bad, lewd fellow, and
"used such speeches of her as were not decent to
"rehearse. Finally, she went to the house of one
"Lady Pelham, of Sussex, and there abode until
"Edward Lovell, now servant to Thomas Clopton,
"administered a potion to William Clopton, which
"was a purgative or such like, from the effects of
"which he died, whereas had it happened during her
"residence with him, she would have been charged as
"accessory to his death."

The

Appendix. 347

The Rejoinder of Thomas Clopton, Efq., and John Bowfell, to the above Replication of Anne Clopton:

"Denies the allegations attributing her leaving to the "indifcreet behaviour of complainant, and unnatural "dealing towards her late hufband, whom fhe neither "loved nor obeyed; condemns the ftatement about "Lovell as flander; depofes to the perfect ftate of "the faculties of William Clopton, and his powers of "memory and appetite, &c."

B—page 16.

It would appear from the mention in this place "between 1563 and 1570," that there is fome uncertainty about the date of fale by W. Bott to W. Underhill, whereas the exact date, Michaelmas Term, 1567, is given with a copy of the Fine at p. 85. The truth is, that when paragraph 3rd, p. 16, was ftereotyped, I had not difcovered the Fine given at p. 85; and rather than cancel the page, I preferred to make the correction in this place.

C—page 19.

The general reader had better be warned, particularly if he fhould be a reader of Malone, againft falling into the error into which that author, in the original edition of his Shakefpere's Works, would betray him.

The ftatement there made, both as to the Nafh pedigree, and as to the manner in which New Place paffed from owner to owner, is completely erroneous. The fact is well known to every Shakefperian fcholar but it may be as well to fet it forth diftinctly. Malone fays—

"Sir

"Sir John Clopton, Knt. (the father of Edward
"Clopton, Efq., and Sir Hugh Clopton), who died at
"Stratford-upon-Avon in April, 1719, purchafed the
"eftate of New Place, etc., fome time after the year
"1685, from Sir Reginald Forfter, Bart., who married
"Mary, the daughter of Edward Nafh, Efq., coufin-
"german to Thomas Nafh, Efq., who married our
"poet's grand-daughter, Eliz. Hall. Edward Nafh
"bought it after the death of her fecond hufband,
"Sir John Barnard, Knt. By her will, fhe directed
"her truftee, Henry Smith, to fell the New Place,
"etc. (after the death of her hufband), and to make
"the firft offer of it to her coufin, Edward Nafh,
"who purchafed it accordingly. His fon, Thomas
"Nafh (whom, for the fake of diftinction, I fhall call the
"younger), having died without iffue in Auguft, 1652,
"Edward Nafh, by his will, made on the 16th March,
"1678-9, devifed the principal part of his property to
"his daughter Mary, and her hufband, Reginald
"Forfter, Efq., afterwards Sir Reginald Forfter; but
"in confequence of the teftator's only referring to a
"deed of fettlement executed three days before, with-
"out reciting the fubftance of it, no particular mention
"of New Place is made in his will. After Sir John
"Clopton had bought it from Sir Reginald Forfter, he
"gave it by deed to his younger fon, Sir Hugh, who
"pulled down our poet's houfe and built one more
"elegant on the fame fpot."

Malone's errors in the above paffage are extraordinary, becaufe they are not only errors as to pedigree, but errors as to fales and purchafes, which the fmalleft amount of inveftigation would have proved to him to have been incorrect. It is eafy to fet him right upon the pedigree, but impoffible to conceive how he could be fo mifled as to make the feries of egregious blunders which will appear in the above extract when it is compared with the correct ftatement, in par. 7, p. 19.

I give the pedigree which was accepted by Stevens and Malone firft, and then the correct one. By the
firft

Appendix.

first it will be seen that it was supposed there was a lineal descendant of Shakespere in the female line; by the second it is apparent that there was no such descent.

If the reader happens to be familiar with the *original* edition of Malone, he will be struck by the discrepancy between my statement, at p. 19, and the statement made by Malone. It will be found on reference to Boswell's edition of Malone, 1821, that the error in the original edition had been discovered, and was corrected by Boswell. Malone had been misled by the incorrect pedigree (No. 1), which had been supplied to Mr. Stevens by Mr. Whalley, upon which Malone had relied. It represented the existence of direct descendants from Elizabeth Nash, Shakespere's granddaughter, and that Sir Reginald Forster, of East Greenwich, married the daughter of Elizabeth and Thomas Nash, thereby coming into possession of New Place. The error arose from mistaking the daughter of Edward Nash, Esq. (A), of East Greenwich—cousingerman of Thomas Nash, of Stratford—and supposing her to have been the child of Thomas Nash, who never had any children by his wife, Elizabeth Hall. To avoid any further errors upon this subject, the reader is cautioned against the statement made in Malone's original edition, which was set right by Boswell in the 1821 edition.

D—page 51.

Jordan.

Gentlemen's Magazine, October, 1800, p. 1000.—
" When Ireland was engaged upon his ' Picturesque
" View of the Avon, he navigated down this poetic
" stream attended by a very modest and well-informed
" man, Mr. John Jordan,' &c. It was Mr. Jordan who
" gave

"gave Mr. Ireland his firſt information on which he created his viſionary falſehood (the Shakeſpere forgeries)."

Ditto, 1809, September, p. 885.—" It is conjectured that many of his (Jordan's) tales reſpecting Shakeſpere were from his own inventive genius."

E—page 57.

The Clopton Arms.

The porch of the Chapel of the Holy Croſs has been allowed to fall into ſuch a ſtate of decay, that only one of the four ſhields which once adorned it can now be read. It is the one bearing the arms of London.

The ſhields, as they originally appeared, are given by Dugdale, and could eaſily be reſtored. A beautiful coat of the Cloptons will be found inſide the chapel, adorning the porch at the entrance. It is unfortunately buried under the clumſy and offenſive gallery which has been erected over the line of the ſcreen which originally divided the chapel from a ſmall ante-chapel. Holy Croſs is one of the moſt painful ſpecimens of plaſterers', painters', and carpenters' church reſtoration. Its pews and fittings are moſt ſubſtantial, moſt ſerviceable, and moſt deteſtable.

It is well known to every one acquainted with the building, that its walls are adorned with a ſeries of freſcoes of the moſt intereſting deſcription. Theſe have been carefully hidden under coats of yellow waſh. Everything that the Corporation of Stratford could do to diſguiſe this venerable pile, has been done. The ancient oak ſcreen has been hidden behind the gallery; the exquiſite ſtonework of the porchway has been mutilated; and all that the moſt barbaric Proteſtant taſte could accompliſh to convert the building into the appearance of a comfortable conventicle, has been
thoroughly

Appendix. 351

thoroughly carried out. There are only three features, internally, of this building, that carry us back in imagination to Sir Hugh Clopton's time. 1ſt. His ſhield and quarterings, which have happily eſcaped deſtruction on one ſide of the doorway. 2nd. The tracery of the windows. 3rd. A beautiful piece of mediæval iron-work—the handle of the prieſts' door, paſſing from the chancel to the garden formerly occupied by the prieſts' houſes, attached to the preſent grammar ſchool.

The ſooner the Corporation of Stratford ſet about a reſtoration of this chapel — clean the walls and reproduce the freſcoes; remove the frightful and uſeleſs gallery blocking up the lovely tower arch; reſtore the ſcreen to its proper place, and fit up the building with open benches and ſtalls—the more it will be to their credit.

Inſtead of introducing the following facts in the Clopton Pedigree, I have reſerved them to be inſerted here. It will have been ſeen that on the death of Mrs. Partheriche, the Clopton Houſe Eſtate paſſed under her will to Charles Boothby Scrimſher, Eſq. (I), who took the name of Clopton. The Pedigree ſhows that he was the ſon of Anne Clopton, who married Thomas Boothby, Eſq., and the heir-at-law of Mrs. Partheriche at her deceaſe. According to the proviſions of that lady's will, in default of iſſue the eſtate was to paſs to Edward Ingram, Esq. (K, Pedigree), the ſon of Barbara Clopton and Aſhton Ingram; and, in caſe of default, to his brother John or his heirs, all of whom were tenants for life. In caſe of no iſſue in any of theſe families, the eſtate was to paſs to one Anthony Clopton, of Ireland, who had perſuaded Mrs. Partheriche that he was deſcended from the Clopton family. C. B. Scrimſher Clopton died 1815, without iſſue; Edward Ingram died 1818, without iſſue; John Ingram died, aged 90, November 20, 1824, without iſſue. The ſaid Anthony Clopton died in like manner without iſſue. The eſtate then came to a Mrs. Noel (L),

(L), a sister of the above C. B. Scrimsher Clopton. She, being next heir to the estate, during its possession by the above-named John Ingram Clopton (for, by the will, every possessor was bound to assume the name of Clopton) sold the reversion to Charles Meynell, Esq., for £10,000 in money, and an annuity of £300 per annum; the £10,000 being to pay the debts of her brother Charles Boothby, who, having been greatly embarrassed, committed suicide.

Charles Meynell, Esq., the purchaser of the reversion, died in 1815, leaving two sons and a widow, Elizabeth, who married Samuel Stoddart, Esq.; and they conjointly, by a decree of the Court of Chancery, sold Clopton House and estate for £50 an acre, the purchase-money (279 acres) amounting to £13,975; the buildings on the estate being further valued at £781. The timber sold for £548; and the Clopton pews, in Stratford church, with two smaller ones, for £100; the Clopton meadow, for £1,500; and the furniture and FAMILY PICTURES IN THE HOUSE, for £55!!! The whole were purchased for £16,959 15s. 6d., by George Loyd, Esq., of Welcombe, Stratford, in October, 1830. Mr. Loyd died in July, 1831, leaving the Clopton and Welcombe estate to his brother, John Gamaliel Loyd, Esq., for his life, and afterwards to his nephew, Charles Warde, Esq., the present possessor. There were some legal difficulties, owing to the non-completion of the purchase prior to Mr. Loyd's death, which were set right by an order in Chancery, but they are of no interest to the public. The above facts furnish those who may be interested in the subject with a correct account of the hands through which the Clopton estate has passed since the extinction of the direct descent, as traced upon the Pedigree, down to the present moment.

F—page 87.

F—page 87.

Underhill.

The hiftory of the fettlement of the Underhill family at Eatington, near Stratford, is curious and amufing. The facts now related are gathered from the elaborate notice of Eatington and of the Shirley family contained in the MSS. of the late Rev. Mr. Warde.

The Pedigree I have given fhows that the Underhills came originally from Wolverhampton. They fettled at Eatington in the firft year of the reign of Henry VIII., owing to John Underhill marrying for his fecond wife one Agnes Porter, of Eatington. This John obtained a leafe for 80 years of the manor of Eatington, from Sir Ralph Shirley, Knight. This was an amorous knight, who married in fucceffion four wives,—the laft in the year 1514. This lady, a daughter of Sir Robert Sheffield, bore him a fon, Francis, who was left fatherlefs in the firft year of his life—January, 1517. Being very much his own mafter, before he was of age this foolifh youth married a widow, the relict of Sir John Congreve, of Stretton, county Stafford, and likewife the daughter of his guardian, Sir John Giffard. The widow Congreve brought with her to her young hufband's home two daughters by her late fpoufe, Elizabeth and Urfula Congreve.

By turning to the Underhill Pedigree, it will be feen that the two fons of Edward Underhill, of Eatington, eventually married thefe two young ladies, and the reader will not be furprifed to hear what followed.

By a leafe, dated April 28, 1541, the above-named Francis Shirley was induced to grant the whole of his ancient Warwickfhire property, except the right of prefentation to the church of Nether Eatington, to Edward Underhill and his eldeft fon, Thomas, for a term of 100 years. This leafe was the caufe of much unpleafantnefs and of a long feries of lawfuits, which were

were not finally determined until the year 1652. The Underhills were accufed of having obtained this valuable leafe of the Shirleys' lands by the procurement of the mother of the young ladies, Dorothy Congreve, who had married Francis Shirley. The following extracts, made from depofitions taken at Shipfton-upon-Stour, illuftrate the times, and the characters of Francis Shirley and his wife :—

"Ralph Brokefby, of Sholbye, in the county of "Leicefter, Efq., being examined, depofed—

"That Francis Shirley did not meddle in the "management of his eftate, only in his horfes, hounds, "and deer in his park at Staunton, wherein he took "great delight; but referred the refidue to be ordered, "and for the moft part to be difpofed of, by the faid "Dorothy his wife, and her friends, who ruled the "fame, and efpecially his hofpitality and houfekeeping, "with great frugality and worfhip, to her fingular com- "mendation, as well for prefervation of his woods, "keeping his houfe in good repair, and all other "things whatfoever. From fuch converfation and deal- "ings as he had with and for the faid Francis Shirley, "and his fon, John Shirley, he judged that Eatington "be now (1613) worth £200 per annum more than "the 40 marks paid for it (by the Underhills). More- "over, he depofeth, that Thomas Underhill, and Eliza- "beth his wife, did make an attempt to have had "from Francis Shirley the Fee farm of the manor of "Eatington for £200 in money, wherein they had "prevailed if they had not been providently prevented "by John Shirley, and further he gave his advice to "John Shirley fo to do."

Defpite the litigation, the fenior branch of the Underhills retained poffeffion of Eatington until the expiration of the leafe, in 1641, when the heir removed to Upthrop, in the parifh of Alderminfter, county of Worcefter.

During the reign of Elizabeth, the profperity of the Underhills was at its height; and it was in Shakefpere's
time

time that they acquired lands in and about Stratford, and in numerous parifhes about Eatington.

Our intereft, in this work, is directed to the junior branch of the family, and therefore the fenior line has not been given in the Pedigree. The founder of this junior line was William (A), (the younger fon of the above-named Edward), who married one of the fifters Congreve—Urfula.

He was the father of William Underhill (B), who purchafed New Place from Bott, and fold it fubfequently to Shakefpere. Concerning thefe perfons, I have gathered fome interefting information, which will fhow their connection with the county, and particularly with Stratford-upon-Avon.

(S.P.O. Domeftic Correfp. Elizabeth, vol. cxxxvii. art. 68, 69).

Art. 68.—"*A Booke of the Names of the Gentlemen and Freeholders in the Countie of Warwick.* 1580."

"Hundred de Kington:
* * * *
Tho. Undrill, gent.
* * * *

"Hundred de Barlichway:
* * * *
Wm. Clopton, Efqr.
* * * *
Wm. Underhill, gent.
* * * *
John Coomes, gent.
* * * *
John Shakefpeare.
* * * *
Thomas Shakfpeare.
* * * *
John Shakfper.
* * * *

Art. 69.—

Art. 69.—Another Book, intituled, "*A Booke of the Names and Dwelling-places of the Gentlemen and Freeholders in the Countie of Warwick.* 1580."

(Under Idlicote, no Underhills are placed; the names of Richd. Hall and Wm. Merſhall occurring only.)

"Allington Inferior:
    * * * *
    Tho. Underhill, gent.
    * * * *

"Stretford-upon-Avon:
    * * * *
    Wm. Claptun, Eſquier.
    * * * *
    John Shaxper.
    * * * *
    Wm. Underhill, gent.
    * * * *

"Rowington:
    * * * *
    Tho. Shaxpere.
    * * * *

The following documents, an abſtract of the will of William Underhill (A), and the will in full of his ſon (B)—Shakeſpere's Underhill—ſeem to me to complete all the information regarding this family which it is neceſſary to publiſh.

G—page 88.

G—page 88.

Abſtract of Will of William Underhill.

(*Vide Pedigree*, A).

WILLIAM UNDERHILL makes his will on the 1ſt day of December, anno. 12 Eliz. (1569), and deſcribes himſelf therein as of "Newbold Revell, in Com: Warr. "Gent."* In the firſt place he expreſſes his deſire to be buried by his dearly beloved wife, in the pariſh of Nether Eatington. He then proceeds to expreſs his intentions as to the diſpoſition of his property, as follows:—To his heir, &c., the third part of all his manors, lands, and tenements; the reſt (the manor of Idlicote being held *in capite*) to his executors, with all "leaſes, goodes, cattell, plate, and houſehold ſtuffe," to fulfil the intents and meaning of his will, and to bring up his children.

He prohibits moſt emphatically to his heirs the alienation of his lands, except for their lives, their wives' lives, or leaſes for xxj years. Prohibits his ſon, W. Underhill, from marrying before the age of twenty-four, without the conſent of his brother Shirley, brother Brokeſby, brother Thomas Underhill, and brother Congreve, or their heirs, &c., &c.

In the event of his ſon dying, or going about to alienate or ſell his lands, he provides that they ſhall paſs

---

* I find that the manor of Idlicote was alienated by Louis Greville to William Underhill (A), in the 10th of Eliz., and that in the following year the same Louis Greville alienated to the same William Underhill the manor of Loxley. It will be observed that on the Pedigree I have described this William (A), as of Idlicote and Loxley, while in his will he describes himself as of "Newbold Revell." The above facts will explain the reason. He was commonly known, when he made his will (1569), as Underhill of Newbold Revell, the Idlicote and Loxley property having been acquired only during the two years previous.

pafs to teftator's brother, John. The properties in the will enumerated are the manor of Idlicote, lands and tenements in Idlicote, Coxley, and Hollington, lands in Kington-Baffet, Barton, Meryden, Alfpathe, and Efenell, in the county of Warwick aforefaid. The teftator mentions a brother Humphrey. Alfo a brother Thomas, and the faid Thomas's fon, Francis (his godfon), as follows :—

"And alfo I do give to my brother Thomas, untell his
"fon Frauncis Underhill my godfon be of the age of
"xxiiij yeres and then only to the faid Frauncis and to
"the heires males of the very body of the faid Frauncis
"lawfully begotten as is aforefaid and with like condi-
"cion and untill fuch time as is aforefaid all my landes
"and tenementes with their appurtenances in Hafelor
"*Stretforde-upon-Aven* and Drayton in the county of
"Warwick and in the parifh of Wolverhampton in
"the county of Stafford" &c.

Two more fons of his brother Thomas are alfo mentioned, viz., George and Humphrey. Alfo Humphrey, fon of his brother John. Teftator mentions by name his three daughters, Dorothy, Margaret, and Anne, to each of whom there is a bequeft of £500.

To his fon William, he leaves his fignet of gold. To each of his daughters "*one* filver fpone;" to Dorothie her mother's wedding-ring and one bracelet of gold; to his fecond daughter, "my late moft loving wife "Newport's* wedding-ringe;" to my youngeft daughter, "a little chain of gold, and one other of my firft "wife's ringes."

Legacies are bequeathed to his brother John's children,

---

* This was his second wife, who had pre-deceased him little more than a year, her will (which was made by license of her husband) having been proved on the 28th of January, 1569. She was the widow of Richard Newport, of Hemingham, by whom she had a son, John, and four daughters, Constance, Elizabeth, Ursula, and Mary.

dren, to his fifter Dalby's children, to his fifter Wykeham's children, and to his fifter Mynofa.

Allufion is made to an Elizabeth Underhill, his goddaughter, his fifter Wynifred's daughters, and his fifter Tamer's daughters. He provides, in the event of any difficulty arifing about the interpretation of his will, that it fhall be referred to the judgment and arbitration of his friend, Sir James Dier, Lord Chief Juftice of the Common Pleas.

He ftrenuoufly urges more than once (reiterating the fame defire at the conclufion) the non-alienation of his lands, and particularly requefts that his daughters do not throw themfelves away in marriage ; and fhould they marry contrary to his determination and appointment, or "offend and myfufe "themfelfes in carnall or adulterous lyvyng and the "fame be duely proved" that then the portions and bequefts allotted them fhall be null and void.

This will was proved at London on the 10th day of April, A.D. 1570, the teftator having departed this life, according to the *inquifition poft mortem,* on the laft day of March preceding.

H—page 90.

The Will of William Underhill. (Vide Pedigree, B.)

" 𝔍𝔫 𝔱𝔥𝔢 𝔑𝔞𝔪𝔢 𝔬𝔣 𝔊𝔬𝔡 𝔄𝔪𝔢𝔫 WILLIAM UNDER-
" HILL of Idlicott in the countie of Warwicke
" Efquier beinge of perfect minde and memorie did as
" well in the fixth daie of Julie anno domini 1597 as
" at divers other tymes or at leaft once in the tyme of
" his ficknes whereof he died make and declare his
" laft will and teftament nuncupative in manner and
" forme followeing or the like in effect viz. Firft he
" revoked all former wills and teftamentes by him
" made

"made or declared and willed that his daughter Do-
"rothie fhold have for her parte five hundred poundes
"and all her jewells and that his younger daughter
"named Valentine fhold alfo have other five hundred
"poundes   Likewife he willed that his eldeft fonne
"Foulke Underhill fhold have all his landes and that
"in regarde thereof if he lived he fhould be charge-
"able to perform all fuch promifes and grauntes as
"fhall at anie tyme hereafter appeare to be made by
"him the faide William Underhill in his life time for
"which he had received monie   And further he
"willed that if the faide Foulke Underhill fhould
"happen to die, then his next heire that fhall inherite
"fhold be chargeable to performe the fame his pro-
"mifes and grauntes.   Alfo he willed that everie of his
"other fonnes fhould have two hundred poundes a peece.
"Likewife he the fame William Underhill declared
"that he had oweinge unto him two thoufande poundes
"for the which he had fpecialties. And that one
"Mafter Baffet owed unto him threefcore and tenne
"poundes for which he had nothing to fhewe.   Laftlie
"he conftituted and appointed Mafter George Sherley
"Efquier and Mafter Thomas Sherley his brother
"executors of the fame his laft will and teftament and
"humblie defired that it wold pleafe them to take
"uppon them the execution thereof.   And this his faide
"laft will and teftament he foe made and by worde
"declared in the prefence of divers credible witneffes.

"Proved at London, on the 9th day of Auguft
  "AD 1597, by the oath of Alexander Serle
  "notary public, the proctor of George Sherley
  "Efq. and Thomas Sherley, the executors
  "above named."

It will be obferved that in the above will of W. Underhill (B), he leaves two members of the Shirley
family his executors; from which we may gather that
the difpute between the Shirleys and fenior branch of
the

the Underhills of Eatington did not affect the junior branch at Idlicote.

For thofe who are fond of church-hunting, and reading heraldic achievements, Eatington offers peculiar attractions. It is the burial-place of the diftinguifhed families of Shirley and Ferrers, and is rich in monumental remains. There are memorials likewife to feveral of the Underhills. Edward Underhill, whofe fons married the twin Congreves, is thus remembered—

" Here lyeth buried under this ftone Edward
" Underhill, fometime gentleman of this Town,
" with Margaret, fometime his Wife: which Edward
" diffeafed this world the fifth day of November,
" A.D. M.D.XLVI.

" *On whofe follys Jhefu have mercy. Amen.*"

Thomas, the eldeft fon of the above, and Elizabeth Congreve, his wife, are alfo held in memory, with a very lengthy infcription, of which the following is but a fmall part. Their monumental virtues are immenfe:

" Here lyeth buried the bodyes of Thomas Under-
" hill, of this Towne, Efquier, and Elizabeth his wife,
" who lived married together in perfect amitie about
" 65 years, and had iffue between them xx children:
" viz. xiii fons, and vii daughters. . . . . She dyed
" 24 Junii, An. D. 1603; and he the 6th day of Octo-
" ber next after. . . . .
" *God they feared: God they ferved: God they loved:*
" *and to God they dyed.*"

As far as this book is concerned, the moft interefting of all the monuments is that of the William Underhill (A) from whofe fon Shakefpere purchafed New Place. The infcription runs as follows ·—

" Here lyeth William Underhill of the Inner
" Temple of London, gentleman: of Edward Underhill,
" Efquier, fecond fon; and Urfula his dearly beloved
" wife

" wife, youngeft daughter of John Congreve of Stret-
" ton, in Com. Staff. Efquier, whofe life was a fpectacle
" unto all honeft, virtuous, and obedient wifes: fhe dyed
" the xiiiith day of May, An : Dom : M.D.L.X.I.

" *Upon whofe fouls Chrift have mercy. Amen.*"

(No date is given of the death of this William Underhill (A) ; but the period is fixed by the proving of his will in April, 1570, as above.)

I—page 131.

De Quincey.

De Quincey's article on Shakefpere in the old edition of the " Encyclopædia Britannica," is probably known to a comparatively fmall number of perfons. Probably had he been alive at this time, and having fuch an article to write, he would not have produced the one in queftion ; probably, alfo, in his complete works, now iffuing from the prefs, and fo beautifully got up, we fhall never find the article in queftion. But the well-worn phrafe is painfully applicable, "*literæ fcriptæ manent.*" Whatever fuch a man as De Quincey might write, is fure to leave its mark ; and therefore, when a giant hits a giant's blow, we muft look for the necef-fary contufion. De Quincey ufed his ftrength to bruife the reputation of Shakefpere ; and it is a very forry apology, when you have disfigured a man, to beg his pardon, and fay you did not intend to hit fo hard.

The refult of De Quincey's article has been precifely what any one might expect. Men who have never read that article, perhaps never heard of it, have received through other channels of information the impreffion made by De Quincey. In this way, minds receive pre-judices which no regret on the part of the writer of an
article

article can prevent. I can quite believe that if De Quincey could, years ago, have torn out from the pages of the Encyclopædia his article on Shakeſpere, he would have done ſo. But that can never be done; and though it be ſuppreſſed in his works, or otherwiſe huddled away, it cannot be obliterated from the pages of the work in which it remains, unaſſailable. For this reaſon I have dwelt upon it, and referred to it, hoping that the attention of thoſe who read theſe pages may thereby be drawn to the ſubject, and that a proper antidote may be adminiſtered to the baneful influence which ſuch an article as De Quincey's has had, and would ſtill have if treated with ſilence. It is far more healthy and more juſt to drag it into the open day, point to its injurious paragraphs, and ſay openly—Theſe words ought never to have been written; they are unjuſtifiable; they are the mere conjectures of a man who muſt have regretted writing them, and who never would have written them had he acquainted himſelf thoroughly with the cuſtoms of the times in which Shakeſpere lived.

I give one extract from De Quincey to ſhow how he wrote, and to explain the tone aſſumed by me in the body of this work.

He is commenting on the marriage bond (pp. 29, 30, 31):—

" What are we to think of this document? Trepi-
" dation and anxiety are written upon its face. . . . .
" As the daughter of a ſubſtantial yeoman, who would
" expect ſome fortune in his daughter's ſuitor, ſhe (Anne
" Hathaway) had, to ſpeak coarſely, a little outlived
" her market. Time, ſhe had none to loſe. William
" Shakeſpere pleaſed her eye, and the gentleneſs of
" his nature made him an apt ſubject for female bland-
" iſhments—poſſibly for female arts. Without imputing
" to this Anne Hathaway anything ſo hateful as a
" ſettled plot for enſnaring him, it was eaſy enough
" for a mature woman, armed with ſuch inevitable
" advantages of experience and of ſelf-poſſeſſion, to
" draw

" draw onward a blushing novice, and, without directly
" creating opportunities, to place him in the way of
" turning to account such as naturally offered.

"Young boys are generally flattered by the conde-
" scending notice of grown-up women," &c. . . . . .
" Once, indeed, entangled in such a pursuit, any person
" of manly feelings would be sensible that he had no
" retreat; *that* would be to insult a woman grievously—
" to wound her sexual pride—and to insure her lasting
" scorn and hatred. These were consequences which
" the gentle-minded Shakespere could not face. He
" pursued his good fortunes, half perhaps in heedless-
" ness, half in desperation, until he was roused by the
" clamorous displeasure of her family upon first disco-
" vering the situation of their kinswoman. For such
" a situation there could be but one atonement, and
" that was hurried forward by both parties, whilst, out
" of delicacy towards the bride, the wedding was not
" celebrated in Stratford, where the register contains
" no notice of such an event." . . . . . . (and much
more to the same effect).

The reader will now understand the emphasis used
in various portions of this book; and will, perhaps,
wonder with me that Shakespere's was not too
honoured a name to be dealt with so flippantly by a
famed author in a great national work.

Let it be said of the above, that it is—every syllable
—an unsupported and degrading conjecture; that the
motives and the acts are the base inventions of De
Quincey's own imagination; and that the man who
uses his pen to hurt the fair fame of the dead in such
a fashion, were he twenty times the author and writer
that De Quincey was, deserves the severest condemnation.

J.—page 148.

J – page 148.

CLOPTON PEDIGREE.

Combe, or Combes.

To work out the Combe Pedigree, and to bring it down correctly to the union between the heirefs Martha Combe and Edward Clopton, has coft me an amount of labour, which none but thofe acquainted with the difficulties of fuch work will give me credit for.

By the courtefy and kindnefs of Herald's College, I was enabled to take a copy of the pedigree contained in "Vincent's Warwickfhire" (1619). This book was prefented by Sheldon to the College in 1684, and is always regarded as a moft truftworthy guide. Having poffeffed myfelf of this, I next confulted all the Vifitations and MSS. at the Britifh Mufeum which would give any light on the fubject, and next I ranfacked the regifters of Stratford Church. I have at laft compiled that Pedigree which will be found on one part of the "Clopton" fheet.

In the main features of this Pedigree I have thought it my duty to accept the authority of Vincent, but I confefs I do fo with great hefitation, being unable (except upon a conjecture which I have embodied in the Pedigree) to reconcile the conflicting evidence of Vincent's MS. and the unbending entries which I find in the Stratford Regifter.

To thofe who are curious in fuch matters this fubject cannot fail to be interefting, and therefore I will go into it fully.

After having gone over the Stratford Regifter with great care, and affifted by Mr. Butcher, the Parifh Clerk, who has revifed all my quotations, I find the following to be the whole of the entries with regard to the Combes family about the dates with which we are interefted.

Marriages.

Marriages.

1561. Auguſt 27.—Johannes Combes, generoſus, et Roſa Cloptonne.

Burials.

1573. April 4.—Jone, filia Johannis Combes.

1575. April 8.—Francis, ſonne to Mr. John Combs.

1576. June 11.—Francis, ſonne to Mr. John Combes.

1577. January 29. — John, ſonne to Mr. John Coombes.

1579. Oct. 14.—Miſtreſs Roſe, wife to Mr. John Combes.

1584. Feb. 2.—Will, ſonne to Mr. John Combes.

1584. May 24.—Miſtreſs Elizabeth, wife to Mr. John Combes.

1614. July 12.—*Mr. John Combes, gentleman.*

We naturally aſk, who was this Mr. John Combes? On turning to the inſcription upon the altar tomb of John à Combe, in the chancel of Stratford Church, we find it terminating in this faſhion. After enumerating the bequeſts of the deceaſed, it concludes,—" Ye wich " increaſe he apoynted to be diſtributed towards the " reliefe of ye almes-people theire. More he gave to " the poore of Stratford Twenty LI."

What does that 51 mean? Can it be intended to denote the age of John à Combe at the time of his death? Probably not; but if not, what poſſible meaning can it have?

The reader will ſoon ſee the intereſt of this inquiry. There is no evidence, that I am aware of, to tell us at

what

Appendix. 367

what age John à Combe died; and there are, unfortunately, fo many Combes in the Pedigree named "John," that we are in great danger of confufing one with another. John à Combe, Shakefpere's friend, is commonly reputed to have been an old man at the time of his death; but he is alfo reported to have been an old bachelor. In a MS. given by Mr. Hunter in his New Illuftrations, we read of "an old gentleman, "a batchelor, Mr. Combe, upon whofe name the "poet," &c., &c.

Affuming that John à Combe was an old bachelor, who was the John with all the children?

The Pedigree fhows us that there was another John Combe, living at Warwick, but he had married one Johanna Murcote, and therefore he could not be the hufband of Rofe Clopton, married in 1561, and dead in 1579, nor yet of "Miftrefs Elizabeth," who died in 1584.

We are driven, therefore, to the neceffity of trying to fhow that one of the *above-named ladies was the wife of John à Combe's father*. This is what Vincent fets forth in his Pedigree, and it is fupported by a note of Malone's. He fays, "Mr. Combe married Mrs. Rofe "Clopton, the youngeft daughter of William Clopton "of Clopton, Efq. [*it was old John who married Rofe* "*Clopton*], Auguft 27, 1561; and therefore was, pro- "bably, when he died, eighty years old."

As Vincent was a Warwickfhire man, and had full opportunity of acquainting himfelf perfonally with the hiftories of the families he catalogued in his Vifitation, we feem bound to conclude that John à Combe's father (John of Stratford) was the hufband of Rofe Clopton. The regifter above quoted fhows that fhe lived in wedlock from 1561 to 1579.

During that period, four children of Mr. John Combe's were interred in Stratford Church, viz., Jone, Francis, Francis, John. They evidently were Rofe Clopton's offspring, and died in infancy; *but of them there is no mention made in Vincent's Pedigree*. I have
           introduced

introduced thefe names with dotted lines, according to heraldic cuftom, to fignify that the defcent is doubtful, though there cannot be any doubt upon the point, becaufe the evidence of the Stratford regifter is overpowering: and therefore in the above omiffions, Vincent's Pedigree at Herald's College muft be fo far incorrect.

But Vincent inftructs us that "old John" took Rofe Clopton for his *fecond wife*, and that his celebrated fon, John à Combe, was the third offspring of the firft marriage with Jocofa, the daughter of Edward Blount, of Kidderminfter. It will be feen, on reference, that there were four children by that marriage. Affuming that Jocofa Blount died the year prior to her hufband's fecond marriage, and that her children were born one year after the other, fhe could not have been married later than 1555 (moft probably the date would be two or three years earlier); and affuming that "old "John" was twenty years of age when he married, it would give his date of birth about 1535. It is moft likely that he was born fomewhat earlier, but as marriages were contracted in very young years in thofe days, we could hardly conjecture his birth as prior to 1532. At the death of his fecond wife, therefore, he would be about 47 years of age, and not at all too old to marry for the third time. That he did fo feems almoft certain, becaufe we are encountered with the entry, in 1584, "Miftrefs Elizabeth, wife to Mr. John "Combes." It is quite poffible that this lady might have been the wife of John à Combe, for at that date he was probably five and twenty years of age. But as John à Combe is univerfally reported to have been an old bachelor, this cannot be correct. We have no alternative, therefore, but to conclude that "old John" did marry for the third time, after the death of Rofe Clopton, and that "Miftrefs Elizabeth" was the mother of the child "Will," who was buried February 2, 1584. It was only three months afterwards that the mother followed the child to the grave, and therefore it appears

probable

Appendix.

probable that the child's birth and death coſt the mother her life alſo. With the entry of "Miſtreſs "Elizabeth's" funeral, all knowledge of "old John," as far as I am acquainted, ends. I am at a loſs to underſtand why Malone gueſſes "old John" as probably "eighty years old when he died," ſimply becauſe he married his ſecond wife, Roſe, in 1561, at which date he was poſſibly about thirty years of age—probably ſomewhat younger. Diſproportionate alliances as to years were not faſhionable in thoſe days; and we can with certainty conclude that "old John" muſt have been a youthful bridegroom when he married Roſe, becauſe, in 1561, ſhe muſt have been quite a girl, ſince her eldeſt brother, William Clopton (C), was only born in 1537, and was therefore but twenty-four years of age when his ſiſter, the third younger than himſelf, was married. Roſe could not have been more than eighteen or nineteen when ſhe married John Combe; and it is not likely that a girl of eighteen, *in thoſe days*, would marry a man many years older than herſelf.

It is quite poſſible that "old John" may have lived until he was eighty years of age. If ſo, he only died four or five years before his ſon, John à Combe. The regiſter of Stratford is totally ſilent on the ſubject, and I can find no trace there of his death or burial. He may poſſibly have been interred at Aſtley, from whence his family came.

It will be ſeen that on the Pedigree I have, with the dotted lines of doubt, ſupplied "old John's" third marriage, and the burial both of his wife and his child, concerning whom Vincent is altogether ſilent. I conclude his Pedigree *muſt be defective,* becauſe the Stratford regiſters will admit of no queſtions or doubts; their entries are abſolute and concluſive evidence.

I confeſs I have had, and ſtill have, ſome doubts as to the correctneſs of Vincent in repreſenting John à Combe as the third child of Jocoſa Blount—"Old "John's" firſt wife; though I dare not venture to call in queſtion his pedigree, becauſe it clears up one

great

great difficulty which has never before been explained, and in this refpect is evidently correct. Thofe who have ftudied John à Combes' Will cannot fail to have been ftruck with the manner in which he confiftently fpeaks of his "brother John and his children," though he alfo fpeaks of his "*Coufin Thomas Combe*," and fubfequently calls him "my faid nephew, Thomas Combe."

"Item. I will and bequeath and devife to my Cousin "Thomas Combe, &c.," .... "that he the faid "Thomas Combe, his heirs and affigns, fhall yearly and "every year for every year for ever pay to a learned "preacher twenty fhillings to make a fermon twice a "year at Stretford Church, &c., &c.," .... "and if "my faid Nephew Thomas Combe .... fhall or "do not pay the faid twenty fhillings yearly to a "preacher," &c.

There can be no queftion as to the perfon here defcribed, nor to the miftake in the drafting of the Will, calling him in the one inftance Coufin, and in the other Nephew.

Having difcovered one fuch miftake, I was led to fufpect that the term "brother" might be alfo open to fome fuch explanation, becaufe, though it was conftantly the cuftom, after the death of one child, to chriften another by the fame Chriftian name (as we fee in the cafe of the infants "Francis," the fons of "Old John"), neverthelefs, we fhould hardly expect to find two brothers living and both bearing the fame title. Vincent's pedigree explains the matter at once. We there fee that thefe Johns, though both fons of "Old John," were, neverthelefs, only *half-brothers*—the one being the child of Jocofa Blount, the other of Rofe Clopton. Hence at their chriftenings each received the name "John;" and when John à Combe was making his Will, it was very natural for him to fpeak of "my brother John."

Having thus fairly acknowledged Vincent's ftrength and authority, I will frankly allow that I have only weaknefs to oppofe to him in fupport of my doubts

and

Appendix.

and hesitations. I have undoubtedly proved one of two things. Either Vincent's Pedigree is incorrect in not having supplied us with the names of Rose Clopton's children in full, and with "Old John's" third marriage, and the name both of his wife and child; or he has altogether dropped out of notice some John Combe, of Stratford, and a member of this family, whose wife and family are proved by the register to have existed.

The difficulty might easily be solved if we entertained the idea of John à Combes having once married—his children having died—and that he was left a widower, instead of being a bachelor. This would make things smooth at once; but unfortunately every sort of evidence and tradition agrees with the pedigree in making John à Combe always and ever a bachelor.

We must conclude, therefore, that Vincent altogether overlooked "Old John's" third marriage. May he not, possibly, have confounded the one John with the other, and have made John à Combe by mistake the son of Jocosa Blount, rather than of Rose Clopton?

There is a strong impression on my mind that I have seen it stated that John à Combe was the son of Rose Clopton. If the figures LI upon his tomb are intended to indicate his age, *he must have been;* for reckoning from 1562, the year after Rose Clopton was married, to the year in which John à Combe died, he would have been 51 at the date of his death, July, 1614; added to which, it must be remarked that Vincent's Pedigree does make a "John Combe" to have been Rose Clopton's eldest child, only it represents him as the "brother John," and makes John à Combe the son of the first wife.

As regards the property or the descent coming down to Martha Combe, wife of Edward Clopton, it matters not whether Vincent is right or wrong. The point is of some interest to those who are endeavouring to put together the facts and associations of Shakespere's day, and to trace out the precise relations of those persons
among

among whom he moved in focial friendfhip and intimacy. As I faid before, I know my pofition is weak, and Vincent's very ftrong. I fubmit, therefore, to his authority, with the ftrongeft inclination to difpute it. When John à Combe died, in 1614, *he could not, under any circumftances, have been an old man.* I cannot calculate him, though the fon of Jocofa Blount, to have been more than fixty at his death. Should it, however, at any time appear that the figures on his tomb denote his real age, it would be a fingular coincidence to find that both Shakefpere and his attached friend died in their fifty-fecond year; and thofe figures would alfo eftablifh the fact that John à Combe came of the Clopton race, *and muft have been the fon of Rofe Clopton.*

K—page 277.

In cafe the reader fhould have a curiofity to fee a houfe exactly like New Place in the laft century, I may mention that the new line of railway between Waterloo Station and London Bridge has lately difclofed one. In paffing along Union Street, in the Borough, in the narrow part, where the feries of arches runs clofe to the back of the houfes on the left (going towards London Bridge), there is a fmall ftreet, called Gravel Lane. In that ftreet I lately came upon the houfe referred to, and as it is precifely fimilar, even in fmall details, to the prints of New Place (1720), it may be an object of intereft to fome of my readers.

As it ftands clofe into the angle where the Chatham and Dover Railway, going to Blackfriars Bridge, croffes the extenfion line from Waterloo to London Bridge, and the Act of Parliament gives powers to purchafe this property, it may be well to draw attention to this interefting old houfe, before the iron Vifigoths fweep it away. It belongs to George Vaughan, Efq., of Weftbourne Terrace, and has been in poffeffion of his

family

family for a conſiderable period. Mr. Vaughan's tenants, J. H. and G. T. James, hatters, have a worthy affection for the old—old place, which ſtands an ancient landmark in the midſt of modern buildings.

Over the doorway, upon a lozenge, is the following inſcription :—

I.
D. H.
1703.

The old leaden tank bears date,
J. C. E.
1669.

The broad ſtaircaſe and the panelled rooms are carefully preſerved, with the exception of the oak out of one of the rooms, which Mr. Vaughan has lately, and very properly, removed to preſerve it, in caſe he ſhould be compelled to part with his cheriſhed houſe. Gravel Lane leads down to the Thames, and to the ſite of the Globe Theatre. The following facts, therefore, become intereſting. Mr. James remembers, when he was a boy, ſome forty years ago, that rows of elm trees ſkirted the lane; and he can recall the fact of an aged carman in the employ of Meſſrs. Vaughan, telling him about the year 1820, that when he was a youth, in taking the carts down to the Thames, he was obliged to puſh the buſhes and brambles out of the way to enable the cart to paſs.

Theſe facts are ſtriking, becauſe they prove that the land behind the Globe Theatre retained the ſame rural character to the end of the laſt century which it muſt have familiarly preſented to the eyes of William Shakeſpere.

There was, until a few months ago, a large garden at the back of Gravel Lane Houſe. It is now being built upon by the piers of the Chatham and Dover railway arches. In it, from time to time, many relics have been dug up. Of courſe there are many houſes around London of the ſame character and date as this houſe, but none in the direction where it ſtill exiſts. I have not, however, ſeen anywhere a houſe

ſo

so exactly corresponding to the elevation of New Place (1720). It is the verisimilitude; and, therefore, if the Londoner wishes to see what New Place was like at that date, he has only (before it is too late) to take a walk over Southwark Bridge, and penetrate the now densely-populated and uninviting heart of the Borough, called Gravel Lane.

L—page 317.

The Rev. R. Jago is buried in the side aisle of the nave of Snitterfield Church, of which he was Vicar. As a poet, he was well and deservedly known about Stratford, and many of his productions obtained a much wider popularity. He lives in the pages of "Elegant "Extracts." One of the best parodies in the English language, upon Hamlet's soliloquy, "To be or not to "be," will be found in that work. It was written by Mr. Jago, and describes the miseries of a would-be poet longing after bays. It commences, "To print, "or not to print," and while adhering most closely to the language of Shakespere, admirably depicts the fears and hopes of the depressed rhymester, working up to this climax—

"Thus critics do make cowards of us all."

Mr. Jago died in 1781, Æt. 69.

HATHAWAY, M.

(See Shakespere Pedigree.)

It appeared to me perfectly unnecessary to encumber the Shakespere Pedigree with the descents of the Hathaways down to their extinction—in the Shottery branch—during the present century. To any one curious on the subject, the Stratford registers will always supply an abundant fund of information.

Appendix.

I have contented myself, therefore, by merely introducing in Shakespere's Pedigree those names which were absolutely necessary to show the connection with him by marriage; and in this place I have collected together such material as seems to me valuable, in order to preserve a correct record of the latest descents of the Shottery family, and of the way in which the property passed from them to its present owner. As no one has previously undertaken to do what I have thus done, I believe that the following information will not only be valuable on the instant, but in some few years hence will become very valuable to the antiquary, who will thank me for rescuing from oblivion many details which in another generation would have been lost for ever. I am under obligation to Mr. William Thompson, of Stratford, the present owner of Ann Hathaway's Cottage, and also to his solicitors, for the prompt manner in which they laid the title-deeds open to my inspection, and for the manner in which they showed themselves anxious to give me any information they possessed. Though Mr. Thompson is yet a very young man, it was exceedingly agreeable to me to find that the Shottery property had come into the possession of a gentleman who thoroughly appreciates its historic associations, and assures me of his intention to preserve the fabric from spoliation or decay. My thanks are also due to Mrs. Baker, of the Cottage, who, I trust, will have no reason to regret the length of time that we puzzled together in her kitchen over the old family Bible, until we got the Pedigree correct, as far as her knowledge went. It must, indeed, be a source of unending regret to this good woman, when she recalls from day to day her father's sale of the house, which belonged for centuries to the long line of her ancestors. It was a bitter necessity; and every visitor to Ann Hathaway's Cottage must feel with her, and for her.

By the help of Mrs. Baker, Mr. Thompson, his lawyer, and the parish clerk, I have been enabled to
put

put together the accompanying Pedigree. By reading it through, and then perusing the abstracts I have made of deeds in Mr. Thompson's possession, the reader will be put in possession of the history of the Hathaway family during the last hundred years.

Abstracts of Title Deeds, &c., regarding Ann Hathaway's Cottage, Shottery.

1.

Will of John Hathaway of Shottery (Pedigree, A).

"Bequeathes to Ursula Good, now Ursula Kamill, "5s., payable 12 months after the decease of my "mother, Sarah Hathaway.

"Also to my sister, Jane Hathaway, now Jane "Webb (B), the sum of Twenty Pounds.

"Also all Freehold Lands, *i.e.* in fee simple, to my "loving mother, Sarah Hathaway, during her life; and "after her decease, I devise the said

"To my three sisters, *Sarah* Hathaway (C), Elizabeth "Hathaway (D), and Susannah Hathaway (E), and "their heirs.

"And I hereby nominate my mother, Sarah Hatha- "way (L), executrix, &c.

"I have hereunto set my seal this 7th day of August, "in the 17th year of the reign of our Sovereign Lord, "George II.

"Proved April 2, 1746."

2.

Will of Sarah Hathaway (C), dated May 3, 1779.

"I give, devise, and bequeath unto my brother-in- "law, William Taylor (F), and Susannah (E), his wife, "during their joint lives, and the life of the longest "liver of them, all that my third part or share of and "in a messuage or tenement, lands, hereditaments, and "premises which I may die seized or possessed of or "entitled unto, situate at Shottery aforesaid, in the "possession of the said William Taylor, or elsewhere—

"and

Appendix. 377

"and from and after the several deceases of the said
"William Taylor and Susannah his wife, then I give,
"devise, and bequeath all and singular the premises
"aforesaid unto my nephew, John Hathaway Taylor (H).
"Proved October 13, 1785, at Worcester."

3.

Conveyance, July 22, 1795—

"Between Richard Standley (G), of Chipping Camp-
"den, County of Gloucester, Flax-dresser, eldest son and
"heir-at-law of Elizabeth Standley (H), his late mother,
"deceased, who was one of the sisters, and a devizee
"named in the last will and testament of Robert
"Hathaway (M), heretofore of Shottery, parish of Old
"Stratford, County of Warwick, Yeoman, deceased,
"and Mary, the wife of the said Richard Standley, of
"the first part; John Hathaway Taylor (I), of Shottery
"aforesaid, yeoman, of the second part; Thomas Hunt,
"of Stratford-upon-Avon, County of Warwick, gentle-
"man, of the third part; in consideration of £55 to
"said Richard Standley, paid by said John Hathaway
"Taylor, the said Richard Standley did convey unto
"said John Hathaway Taylor, all that one undivided
"third part or share, the whole into three equal parts
"to be divided, of and in all those two several cottages
"or tenements, and two orchards, &c. &c., situated in
"Shottery, aforesaid.

"Conveyed in fee to John Hathaway Taylor."

4.

Fine, Michaelmas Term, 36 George III.—

"Between Thomas Hunt, gentleman, plaintive,
"Richard Standley, and Mary his wife, to bar dower."

5.

Will of John Hathaway Taylor (I), dated July 18, 1816.

"John Hathaway Taylor, of Shottery, Lime-burner,
"bequeathes unto my wife, Mary Taylor (J), and her
"assigns,

"assigns, for and during the term of her natural life,
"all those my several messuages or tenements, &c.,
"situate lying and being in Shottery, parish of Old
"Stratford aforesaid, and now in my own and Samuel
"Bridges' occupation as tenant thereof to me; and
"from and after the decease of my said wife, I give
"and devise the said messuages, &c., unto my son,
"William Taylor (L), his heirs and assigns for ever.

"Proved, 9th September, 1820."

6.

Mortgage, January 5, 1836.

"William Taylor (K) to Thomas Talker; mortgage
"of Houses and Premises at Shottery, for securing
"£100 and interest.

(W. S.)

7.

Conveyance, October 30, 1838—

"By William Taylor (K) and the Mortgagee to Mr.
"Thomas Barnes, in fee of two messuages, orchards
"and gardens and premises, at Shottery, parish of Old
"Stratford, County of Warwick. William Taylor re-
"ceived £245, consideration money, and Thomas
"Talker, the mortgagee, £100 from Mr. Thomas
"Barnes, of Luddington."

8.

Mr. Thomas Barnes, by will, dated January 5, 1855—

"Devised all those three cottages or tenements—
"formerly Hathaways—and situated in Shottery afore-
"said, unto William Thompson, his heirs and assigns
"for ever."

Baptism,

Appendix.

Baptifm, 1747.—December 18, John Hathaway, fon of William Taylor.

1809.—John Taylor and Elizabeth Barnett, married, January 3, at Stratford.

1828.—September 5, John Taylor, buried, aged 49.

1835.—January 10, Mary Taylor, aged 82.

I append a few entries from the Marriage Regifter of Stratford which are not familiar; though attention has been previoufly drawn to that of Jan. 17, 1579, when one William Wilfonne married one "*Anne Hathaway of Shotterye.*"

The extracts from churchwardens' accounts I have not feen before in print. Thefe accounts are full of the names and fignatures of perfons with whom we are familiar as living in Shakefpere's time.

Marriage Regifter, Stratford.

1567. January 13.—Lawrentius Walker et Phillippa Hathaway.

1570. October 22. — George Hathaway et Anne Catan, of Loxley.

1572. May 18.—Henry Smith, of Banbury, to Ales Hathaway, of Shottery.

1575. Thomas Hathaway et Margaret Smith.

1579. *January 17. — William Wilfonne et Anne Hathaway, of Shotterye.*

June 22.—David Jones et Ffrances Hathaway.

1634.—Regifter figned by John Hathaway, churchwarden.

Churchwarden's Accounts.

1633. July 18.
        Signed, Tho. Nafhe.
"A Levy of Taxation" . . . . . of £40 throughout the whole parifh.

The

The account of William Walford, ... April, 1618, churchwarden for the year paſt. Borough of Stratford:

"Henley St. Ward.
" Received of Rich. Hathaway . . iij$^{s.}$ iiij$^{d.}$"

Sept. die. Junii, Anno 1619.
Accounts ſigned, Richard Hathway.

The fifteenth of April, 1628.
Mr. John Hall, Churchwarden for the Borough.

7th day of April, 1629.
Surveyors for the highways.
George Barker, } for the County.
John Hathaway,

24th day of February, 1627.
Will. Combe.
Ge. Combe.
Richard Hathaway.

8th day of October, 1626, } R. Hathaway, Bayliffe.
27th March, 1627.

3rd day of April, 1621.
Batholomew Hathaway,
George Quiney, Curat.

Ditto, April, 28, 1620.

Oct. 17, 1641. Tho. Clopton.

The name of Barnard appears frequently.

FINIS.

J. S. Virtue, Printer, City Road, London.